TRUE TALES
To Live By

Best Wishes,
Skip

Skip Westphal

Dageforde Publishing, Inc.

Copyright 2002 Clarence A. Westphal. All rights reserved. No part of this publication may be reproduced, stored in a retrieval system, or transmitted in any form or by any means, electronic, mechanical, photocopied, recorded, or otherwise, without the prior written permission of the publisher.

ISBN: 1-886225-83-4
Cover design by Angie Johnson

Dageforde Publishing, Inc.
128 East 13th Street
Crete, Nebraska 68333
Ph: (402) 826-2059 FAX: (402) 826-4059
email: info@dageforde.com

Visit our website: www.dageforde.com

Printed in the United States of America
10 9 8 7 6 5 4 3 2 1

*Dedicated to my loving wife Marion
and our daughters Kimberly and Sunia*

Contents

Introduction ix
A Monument to a Duck 1
Cher Ami Hero of the Battle Front 3
An African Mother Faces a Lion 4
A Lion Cub and a Burglar 7
The Little Chicken in the Woodpile 9
Skippy's Christmas Surprise 11
The Seeing-Eye Duck 13
A St. Bernard Dog's Famous Rescue 17
The Loving Bull Moose 18
A Dog Finds a New Home 19
A Child Saved by an Elephant 24
The Tramp and the Little Black Dog 25
Buster and the Angry Bull 28
The Tiger and the Puppy 30
A Dolphin to the Rescue 32
A Strange Dog Was her Protector 34
A Mule Saved his Life 36
Under the Big Top 38
Give Her a Lot of Propaganda 40
Something like Teaching School 41
We Take to the Road 42
Some Strange Bedfellows 43
When Dreams Come True 44
Leaving Old Circus Friends 44

PIONEER DAYS

Trapped by a Prairie Fire 49
Some Early Prairie Farmers Lived in Caves 51
The Strenuous Life of a Pioneer Homemaker 52
Traveling by Wagon Train 55

An Unexpected Visitor 57
Soddies Provided Primitive Shelter 58
Traveling by Stage Coach 60
Chief White Pigeon, Heroic Indian Chief. 62
Chief Black Hawk, Fighter for Indian Rights 63
Friendly Wolf. 66
Massacre Threat at Fort Madison 68
The Battle of Bloody Creek 70
Southern Swamps: Beautiful but Dangerous 72
The Buffalo Hunt 76
Pioneers Had Reason To Be Thankful 77
Pilgrim Encounters Stormy Sea in 1620 79
Thirty-Nine Indians Hanged on a Single Scaffold 81
Boom Towns of the West 82
Honeymoon Almost Ends in Disaster 83
Murder Not a Crime? 85
Indians a Threat to Pioneer Preachers 86
On a Trap Door to China 90
The Little Professor of Piney Woods 92
The Little Professor Is Taken from his Church 94

AFRICAN ADVENTURES

A Visit to the Land of the Little People 101
Medicines from Poison Arrows 103
Little Children of the Forest 110
Pygmies Build Airport in the Jungle 111
A Beggar Girl on the Streets of Cairo 113
Hitchhiking a Ride on a Camel 116
A Meeting with a Puff Adder 117
Chased by a Lion 119
A Call on the King of the Bakubas 121
Black Mamba Captures Thief. 123
What Africans Can Teach Us. 124
Apollo Mweja 126
Mooney, the Pet Lion 128
What Africa Gives To Us 134
Perfumes from Africa 138

By Riverboat up the Congo. 140
The Palm Trees of Brabanta 142
The Fabulous Gold Mines of Johannesburg. 145
Acres of Diamonds. 147
Cobalt, a Nuisance Metal? 154

INTERESTING PEOPLE WHO HAVE CROSSED MY PATHWAY

Don't Saw Off that Leg 159
The Friendly Cobbler 160
Was This Man a Failure? 161
John Wayne Inspired a Song. 163
Grandmother to over 100 Thousand Orphans. 164
Okotambulu and the Elephant 169
The Lost Wedding Ring 171
An Inspiring Poster in a Restroom 172
Meeting with Joni Eareckson 174
The Amazing Story of Bob Wieland 175
Was the Appearance of a Patrolman a Coincidence? 178
A Veteran Recalls Days on the Battlefield. 180
The Chinese Cake Peddler 183
Home from Peru on Crutches 184
The "Good Doctor" of Lambarene 187
The Stranger on the Moscow Subway 192

STORIES THAT TOUCH THE HEART

A Shepherd Calling His Lost Sheep 197
Saved By a Smile 199
I Want To Buy a Miracle. 200
A Boy's Sense of Humor. 202
What If the Lady Had Caught that Bus 203
John Wayne's Response to a Young Girl's Letter. 205
The Handwriting on the Wall. 206
The Handwriting on the Wall. 208
The Little Girl at the Window 209
A Surprise Christmas Gift 210
This Is Jim Checking In 213
A Small Gift of Love. 215

The Tiger and the Wise Man 217
The Lost Bible 218
Something for Stevie 219
The Organ Grinder 223
Tolstoy and the Beggar 225
The Old Country Church 226
How the Great Guest Came 228

BITS OF HUMOR

Laugh and the World Laughs with You 233
Three Monkeys 235
Kiddie Quotes 237
The Ram Had a Sense of Humor 238
The Queen Passing By 239
Humor Lightened Burdens Faced by our Forefathers 242
Snake in the Clothes Basket 243
Physical Fitness Not Needed 244

About the Author 245

Introduction

The search for buried treasure has always been an exciting adventure. Millions of dollars have been found at the bottom of the Caribbean Sea, recovered from ships that have been sunk by pirates or lost during storms.

This kind of treasure is only available to those involved in searching for it. There is another treasure that does not consist of gold coins and precious stones. I have found it in the inspiring experiences of men and women I have met in my travels in sixty countries around the world. These people have shared with me over 1700 inspiring stories. I have put together 120 of my favorites in this book.

It is my hope that the readers of these stories will not just read them, then put them on a shelf to gather dust, but will look for opportunities to share them with others.

A Monument to a Duck

In the small suburb of Freiburg, Germany, there stands an unusual monument, a five-foot high statue of a duck.

There have been many statues of war heroes such as General Jackson on horseback in Jackson Square in New Orleans. There are statues of children, like the one in Omaha in Boys' Town of an older boy carrying a small boy on his back with the inscription, "He's not heavy, he's my brother." Millions of people have admired the beautiful statue of Abraham Lincoln in Washington, D.C. but what could be the reason for a statue of a duck? Here's the story.

During World War II, the people of the city of Freiburg, Germany, were fearful of air raids. Often when enemy planes dropped bombs on the city, many of the people were unable to run to the air raid shelters in time to escape the bombs.

The inhabitants of a small suburb of the city had a bit of extra protection from enemy planes. Some of the people noticed a duck running down the street, squawking loudly, shortly before the first air raid hit the city. Evidently, the duck had sensed that the enemy planes were coming before the air raid sirens sounded. Can you imagine the people of that town depending on a duck for their safety?

That duck was obviously an unusual duck, quite different from the other ducks in that town. He loved the children in his neighborhood for often he could be seen waddling out on the street to watch the children at their play.

All of the people, young and old, had a deep affection for that duck because of his rare ability to sense the approach of enemy planes.

What is rather unusual about that duck is that his owners evidently trusted him to be free to wander out on the street, instead of keeping him penned in the back yard.

TRUE TALES To Live By

He may have been a *house duck*, permitted to come into the house where his owners lived. In fact, I once knew a family in Canada; the owner was a blacksmith, who had a pet duck. They also had a dog that barked when the duck wanted to enter the house. When the duck was in the house and wanted to go out, he would squawk. You would think he would make a mess in the house, but he seemed to have good manners.

This German duck may have been like that Canadian duck. We know he was allowed to roam the streets as he wished or he wouldn't have been able to sound the alarm when he heard enemy planes approaching. When the people were alerted to the approach of the bombers, one of the children would always pick up the duck and carry him to the bomb shelter where he would be safe.

One day, the children in the neighborhood who were playing in their back yard heard that duck squawking loudly as he ran down the street.

"The planes are coming! The planes are coming!" they shouted. In minutes, the street was swarming with people running for the nearest bomb shelter. Mothers with babies in their arms were crying, "the planes are coming!" What pandemonium!

Fortunately, most of the people reached the bomb shelters in time before the bombs began to fall. Many of the houses were destroyed in that raid.

When the planes had passed over, the people began to emerge from their shelters. Houses in the town were burning, others were completely destroyed, but almost all of the residents had escaped the raid.

Immediately the people began to inquire about the duck. Some of the children searched frantically for him. Finally, they found him near the entrance to one of the shelters. He was dead! In their hurry to escape the bombs, no one thought to pick up the duck.

Some of the children dug a small grave for him and many tears were shed as they stood around it. The whole town mourned the death of that war hero.

As the days passed, many of the townsfolk still were talking about that air raid and how their friend had lost his life warning them of the danger that threatened them. One day, someone suggested that a monument be erected in his memory.

Some scoffed at the idea. "A monument to a duck? Who ever heard of a monument being erected to a duck?"

Others thought it would be a good idea, and finally a collection was taken to hire a sculptor to work on the statue.

When it was completed, a day was set for a ceremony for its unveiling. As the townsfolk gathered around, the mayor made a speech that was long to be remembered.

He said: "It is stupid to hate one's brother. This monument is a symbol of the respect due to all creatures of God."

Sometimes, it seems as if animals and our feathered friends act more like human beings should than people do themselves! If people followed the teachings of the Prince of Peace, there would be no more wars and no more terrible bombings like the ones that destroyed the city of Freiburg.

Cher Ami Hero of the Battle Front

Many people probably are not aware that homing pigeons were used to carry messages during wartime. It is interesting to know that these amazing pigeons can fly at altitudes of thirty-five thousand feet, where humans would need oxygen masks. They can withstand temperatures of thirty-five degrees below zero.

The most famous pigeon in World War I was *Cher Ami*. He was called a hero for he saved the lives of an entire American battalion, which was trapped behind enemy lines and completely surrounded by German forces.

Cher Ami had been assigned to a battalion of the Seventy-seventh Division in the Argonne Forest near Verdun. The pigeon was transported on a motorcycle in a

TRUE TALES To Live By

basket under cover of night. The basket was covered with wire as protection from large trench rats. Sometimes these pigeons were dropped by parachutes to beleaguered enemies.

The lost battalion had run out of food, lost a fourth of its men and had no medic left to treat the wounded. Sergeant Richards, the pigeon handler, had only one pigeon left in the basket.

He sent Cher Ami up with a message for help attached to its leg. It had to fly in a circle several times to get its bearings. This gave the Germans the opportunity to take shots at him.

He was shot down three times, but each time rose again into the air. Twenty-five minutes later, the instinct of returning to home uppermost in his throbbing heart, he reached his own loft. One eye had been shot out, his breastbone shattered, and a leg was missing. When that pigeon was sent aloft, the soldiers in that lost battalion prayed for that little bird, some who probably had never prayed before. They knew that their lives depended on his being able to keep flying in spite of the enemies' bullets.

No wonder they gave the pigeon that name, Cher Ami, the French name for *dear friend*, for he was their soldiers' dear friend.

An African Mother Faces a Lion

A group of boys and girls was playing near the edge of a forest in Africa. Their home was a jungle village of grass huts where their mothers were preparing supper.

Suddenly the women heard a frightened scream from the children.

"Help!" they called out. "Help us! Rebecca has been attacked by a lion!"

Leaving their cooking pots, the women ran toward the frightened children who were waving their arms and running toward the women with the tears streaming down their faces.

"Where is Rebecca?" one of the women called out. "I don't see her!"

"Over there by that big rock," one of the children sobbed. "The lion is carrying her off toward the forest like a cat carries her kitten."

The mother of Rebecca was running ahead of the others. Suddenly she cried out, "I see her. The lion has her in his mouth! Drop that child! Drop that child!" she screamed as she ran toward the lion.

The beast heard her cry, for he suddenly stopped and put the sobbing little girl down on the grass. Then he turned to face the mother, showing his teeth in an angry snarl.

The mother slowed down to a walk. Without saying another word, she advanced slowly toward the lion. Now she was only a few feet away. Again the lion let out an angry snarl and the mother stopped almost paralyzed with fear.

"Oh, Dear God!" she prayed. "I can't do it! Give me courage to face that lion!" Then she dropped slowly to her knees and with hands clenched in prayer she whispered, "You closed the mouth of the lion for Daniel. Please do it for me. Please save my child!"

The lion seemed to be puzzled by the woman's action, and still staring at her, he backed up a few steps and sat down. In the meantime, the children and the women who had been following dropped to their knees and were praying with tears streaming down their cheeks.

Suddenly there came to the mind of the agonizing mother the words of the prophet Isaiah that their Christian missionary had taught them and the children to memorize in Sunday school: "Fear not for I am with thee. Be not dismayed for I am thy God. I will strengthen thee, I will help thee, I will uphold thee with the right hand of my righteousness."

TRUE TALES To Live By

As those words crept into her mind, something miraculous happened. The fear that had gripped her heart suddenly faded away.

Repeating those words in a calm tone of voice, she slowly rose to her feet and moved toward her child who was lying on the grass, trembling with fear. Soon, she was close enough so she could stoop and gather her sobbing daughter in her arms. Then with her eyes still firmly fixed on the lion, she began slowly to back up. As she did so, the beast stood up and crept toward her. She stopped. When she stopped, the lion stopped. She started to back up, and again the lion moved toward her. But whenever she stopped, the lion stopped.

After several of these threatening moves, a miracle happened. Suddenly the beast slowly turned and walked away toward the bushes. A moment later, he disappeared into the forest.

As the mother ran toward the women and children who had been watching this frightening incident, one of them cried out, "How could you do it, Mother? How could you do it?"

"The Lord gave me the courage," she sobbed as they all gathered around and threw their arms about the mother and her child. "The words, 'fear not for I am with thee' came to my mind and all fear suddenly left me. Something in my heart seemed to tell me that my God and I were braver than that lion. The Lord saved both Rebecca and me. I shall thank Him and praise Him as long as I live!"

The people of the village were deeply moved by this amazing incident. With their talking drums, they spread the news for miles around of how, inspired by the words of the Bible, that mother had saved her child from the jaws of the lion.

A Lion Cub and a Burglar

John Dodgen, a lover of exotic animals, from Humboldt, Iowa, adopted a lion cub that he named Zaki. She was a loving pet for his children. They kept it in their house and it was as gentle and loving as their pet dog. Zaki would play games with the children although she sometimes got into an argument with the cat over its food dish.

When John came home from work in the evening, Zaki was usually waiting on the stairs of the Dodgen home to welcome him. As he opened the door, the little lion jumped into his arms to greet him.

One evening at the supper table, John had a disturbing announcement to make. "The *town fathers* have decided that no one living in the city limits is permitted to keep a wild animal on his premises. That means that we will have to get rid of Zaki."

The children were very sad at the thought of losing their favorite pet, but they knew that if it were against the law to keep her, their father had no choice but to sell or give her away. Mr. Dodgen finally gave the lion to a friend in Indianola, Iowa. This city did not prohibit keeping a lion in town. That little lion was as much a pet in his new home as he had been in the Dodgen household.

One Christmas Eve, the children were all seated on a couch near the brightly decorated tree. As always on this festive occasion there was a pile of presents.

Mary Lou Dodgen posing with her pet cub.

TRUE TALES To Live By

Everyone was anticipating the happy moment for the sharing of gifts. Zaki was sitting on the couch with them. She was now a bit bigger than she had been in the Dodgen home but just as gentle and as loveable.

Suddenly, the door was flung open and there appeared, not the Santa Claus everyone expected, but a masked man with a gun. The frightened children and their mother sat there amazed and petrified with fear.

"Up with your hands!" the burglar shouted. "This is a holdup!"

Zaki was the only one who was not frightened. She was obviously angry at this sudden intrusion. With an angry growl, she jumped from the couch and leaped upon the robber who fell on his back, his gun flying from his hand. Zaki stood over the burglar with her mouth inches from the man's face. Lucky for the intruder, Zaki didn't sink her teeth into the man's face but stood over him with one paw on the man's chest.

Hearing the burglar's angry shout, the father rushed in from an adjoining room and was amazed to see a man on the floor with Zaki standing over him.

"Please," the burglar pleaded with a frightened look. "Call off this animal!"

The father stood there for a moment with a smile on his face. Then reaching for the telephone, he replied calmly, "I think I'll let the police take care of this situation." Then he said over the phone, "There's a burglar in my house but I'm holding him. Get over here and arrest him." Then to Zaki he ordered, "You just stay there, keep that fellow on his back!" The lion stood still with her chin on the prostrate man's chest, occasionally uttering a menacing growl.

Imagine the look of surprise on the policemen's faces when they entered the house and saw a man lying on his back, held there by a lion. In all their experience, they had never made an arrest in such a situation.

When this unusual event was taking place, John Dodgen was in San Francisco on a business trip. As he came downstairs from his hotel room, he picked up the morning paper.

As he sat down for breakfast, he was amazed to see a newspaper headline reading, "Lion Captures Burglar." Noting that the news item originated in Indianola, Iowa, Mr. Dodgen exclaimed, "That must have been Zaki!" Then as he read the newspaper article, he exclaimed excitedly, "It was! That was my Zaki!"

That lion made history. There probably was not another lion that had ever captured a burglar.

A lion cub like Zaki can be a loving pet. It is not advisable, however, to have an almost full-grown lion for a pet. A lion is, at heart, a wild animal, and may attack a person without warning.

Zaki, however, was an exception. The last word about this unusual lion was that now full-grown, he had been bought by a rancher in Texas. The lion loved to ride in the back of a pickup like a pet dog while his owner was occupied with the task of checking his cattle.

The Little Chicken in the Woodpile

During the years prior to World War II, I was involved in counseling with boys. I was often impressed by the influence of animals on their character.

One of the most delightful stories I have to tell is about a boy who was sent to a home for so-called *problem* boys.

Most of the boys had their hobbies. Some had cats for pets. Others liked dogs. One boy had a pet pig. Most of them loved baseball, others preferred horseback riding. While most of those boys had their special hobbies, there was one who seemed uninterested in anything. The other boys tried to get Jimmy to go fishing and swimming, but he wasn't interested. The members of the staff at the farm tried every means they could think of to bring Jimmy out of his shell but without success.

TRUE TALES To Live By

When one of the cows excited the boys by giving birth to a calf, Jimmy paid no attention. When a cute little colt made its appearance in the barn, Jimmy didn't even notice it. This lad was the saddest, gloomiest boy you could possibly imagine. He was never known to smile. The home psychiatrist feared that this boy would someday have to be sent to a mental hospital.

One day, Jimmy was wandering about the yard near the barn when he heard a plaintive cheep behind the woodpile. He soon discovered that it came from a fluffy, white chick that had lost its way. He picked it up and took it to Pete Wilson, the farmer in charge of the animals.

"Where did you find that chick?" Pete asked in surprise.

"It was lost in the woodpile," Jimmy answered. "Can I keep it for a pet?"

Pete's eyes lit up, and slapping Jimmy on the shoulder he exclaimed, "Of course you can Jimmy. Take it to the hen house if you like and give it some feed." Then he had a happy thought, "Would you like to be in charge of the other little chicks and the hens in the hen house? You could feed and water them and gather the eggs. Wouldn't that be fun?"

Jimmy looked at the little chick in his hand and then with a smile he replied, "Yeah! I think I'd like that."

Pete was delighted. Had the boy come out of his shell like the chicken he held in his hand?

From that day on, Jimmy was a changed boy. He loved those chickens and soon became friends with everyone at the farm as he shared with them his delight with his new job. He was proud of his reputation as the *Chicken Boy* at the home.

A miracle had taken place in that boy's life. The workers at the home had worked so hard and prayed so long for a miracle to happen in Jimmy's attitude. And it did, in a way they didn't dream of—through a little chicken lost in a woodpile.

SKIP WESTPHAL

Skippy's Christmas Surprise

There was a knock at the door. "I'll get it," Bob called out. "Maybe it's another Christmas present!"

A moment later he returned shouting excitedly, "It is another Christmas present! A box of delicious chocolates! Shall I sample them?"

"No, Bob," his mother interrupted. "Let's wait until after the program at the church; then we can all have some."

"Well, OK," Bob grumbled as he put the box under the Christmas tree, "but they look so good!"

Bob was one of the three children of Glenn and Ruth Swartzendruber who operated a grain elevator near Manson, Iowa. Glenn was so well liked by the farmers who brought him grain that many of them gave the family presents at Christmastime. The other member of the family was a Shetland Sheep dog called Skippy. Skippy loved all of the family except for Glenn. Glenn sometimes teased the little dog, and Skippy, like children, didn't like to be teased.

The children's Mom sometimes placed a piece of candy on each child's pillow at bedtime as a reward for good behavior. That was probably one of the reasons that they were usually quite well behaved.

When the family returned from the Christmas program at the church that night, Glenn unlocked the door, and Bob was the first to dash into the room to help himself to the box of chocolates.

Suddenly he called out, "Hey! Look at this! There are four pieces of candy missing from the box!" Then turning to Skippy, he put his hands on his hips and demanded sternly, "Skippy, did you steal those chocolates?"

Poor Skippy was crushed. No one ever spoke to him in such a scolding tone of voice. He meekly crawled under a chair and resting his chin on his paws, he looked very sad.

In the meantime, Kathy who had gone to her room suddenly called out, "Look at this! There is a piece of

TRUE TALES To Live By

chocolate on my pillow! And there's a piece on Mary's pillow, too!"

Then Bob ran to his room and, sure enough, there was a piece of candy on his pillow.

Now Ruth became curious and she had to go to her room to investigate.

"Can you believe this?" she exclaimed. "There's a piece of candy on my pillow!" Then she added with a laugh, "There's none on Dad's pillow!"

On investigating the pieces of candy, they found a tiny hole on each side where Skippy had picked it up very carefully so as not to crush it.

But the laugh was on Dad. He got nothing!

In the midst of the excitement, Kathy inquired, "Where is Skippy? We must thank him for this!"

"He's hiding under the chair!" Bob exclaimed. "Poor Skippy? I blamed him for eating the candy! I've got to apologize to him."

Running over to Skippy, who still lay crouching under the chair, Bob took him in his arms and said gently, "Poor Skippy! I'm sorry I scolded you. We should all thank you for the nice thing you did."

Then as they all gathered around to pet the little dog, Dad remarked, "I just got what I deserved. I'm sure we all know that when we give love, we get love in return, whether it be to a dog or a human being."

"Bob has shown us something, too," Mom remarked. "If we accuse somebody wrongly, even if it's an animal, we should apologize for it, as Bob has done. See Skippy wagging his tail. He won't hold a grudge against Bob like some people do when someone has done them wrong."

The Swartzendruber family always remembered that unusual act of thoughtfulness on the part of their dog. For many years after that they told and retold to their friends, the delightful story of Skippy's Christmas surprise.

SKIP WESTPHAL

The Seeing-Eye Duck

A ten-year-old-girl by the name of Cindy had a very unusual experience with her pet duck. Her father had told her that when Bertha the cow had her next calf, she could consider it her birthday present. Her duck Herman followed her around the barnyard and out into the meadow when she went to the pasture to bring the cows home at night.

Often when she lay down in the shade of a tree by the brook that ran through the pasture, Cindy talked to Herman. He usually sat with his bill resting on her foot and listened to her as if he understood every word.

"Just think, Herman," she said to him one day, "soon Bertha will have a little calf and it will belong to you and me. Won't we have fun with it? We'll call it Betsy, if it's a girl, and Tiny Tim if it's a boy."

Herman blinked his eyes and Cindy knew that he was as excited about that calf as she was.

The day finally came for the big event. Cindy was still asleep one morning when her father brought the news.

"Cindy," he called from the foot of the stairs that led to her bedroom. "Get dressed and come down. I have news for you!"

It didn't take Cindy a minute to get into her dress and come bounding down the stairs.

"Did Bertha have her calf?" she cried out excitedly.

"Yes, Honey," her father replied as he slipped his arm around her, "but I must tell you something that will make you a bit sad. Promise me you won't cry."

"No, I won't cry," Cindy said softly, with a catch in her voice. "Is the calf alive?"

"Yes, it's alive," her father replied, "and it's a beautiful calf. It's black with white spots and it's having its breakfast right now."

"Then why should I feel sad?" Cindy inquired with a puzzled expression.

Her father looked at her sympathetically.

TRUE TALES To Live By

"Let's go out to the barn and you can see."

Without waiting for her father to take her by the hand, Cindy ran out to the stable and peered through the gate into Bertha's pen. She watched for a few moments as the calf eagerly nursed from its mother. Finally, she called to it and when it turned to look at her, she knew why her father had seemed to be so sad. The little calf was blind!

Tears welled up in Cindy's eyes and slowly tricked down her cheeks. She had looked forward so long to the birth of that calf! Now it had come and the poor thing couldn't even see! Then she felt her father's arm about her. "You said you wouldn't cry," he said gently, "but maybe you'll feel better if you do."

As he knelt beside her in the straw, she lay her head on his shoulder and sobbed. "It's such a beautiful calf, Daddy. I wish it weren't blind!"

"Well, aren't you thankful that the calf wasn't born dead? That often happens, you know."

"Yes, Daddy," she said as she wiped the tears from her cheeks with the red bandana handkerchief which he offered to her. "I would rather have a little blind calf than no calf at all, and look who has come to join us."

It was Herman the duck who had waddled into the stable and plopped down beside Cindy. He rested his bill on her foot and he really did look like he was sorry, too, about the little blind calf.

Cindy smiled through her tears and gently stroking the duck's back, she said softly, "You know when a girl needs a friend, don't you Herman? I'm thankful that I have you and we'll take good care of Tiny Tim, won't we?"

"That's the spirit," her father remarked with a sigh of relief. "I knew you would be a good sport and make the best of this situation. I am sure that you and Herman will have a lot of fun taking care of that beautiful calf."

Several days passed and then one morning Cindy's father announced at the breakfast table that it was about time for Bertha to be turned out to pasture.

"If the calf goes with her," he said, "Tiny Tim will have trouble. You know what will happen if he tries to nurse from the wrong cow? The cow will butt him and you wouldn't like that. Then, too, since he can't see, the calf will be running into fences and he could get hurt. Why don't you start feeding him from a bucket?"

"That's a good idea," Cindy exclaimed excitedly. "We can build a pen for him south of the barn so he can enjoy the sunshine."

"I'm all for that," her father replied. "Let's get right to it after breakfast."

Before the day was over, the pen was built with a little shed where Tiny Tim could sleep at night and stay under cover when it rained. Herman had been sleeping in the barn, but now he decided that he would keep the calf company, so often he wriggled under the gate and spent much of his time with the calf in his pen.

Every day when Cindy got home from school, she helped her father with the farm chores; then she went for a walk with Tiny Tim who followed her around the barnyard. Herman tagged along, too, giving a cheerful squawk every few steps he took.

What bothered Cindy was that during the day, instead of running around the pasture like the other calves, Tiny Tim had to lie all day long in his pen. How lonely and tiresome that must have been!

One evening just as Cindy was about to sit down to the supper table, her father came to the door and called out excitedly, "Cindy come here quickly! When I opened Tim's gate to check on him, I forgot to close it and he is out of his pen!"

Cindy ran to the door and, to her surprise, there was Tiny Tim at the far end of the barnyard, but he wasn't alone. Herman was leading the way and the calf was following close behind.

"Isn't this exciting?" Cindy's father exclaimed. "Herman has become a seeing-eye duck! Just as many blind people have seeing-eye dogs, Tim has a seeing-eye duck!"

TRUE TALES To Live By

The next day, Cindy left the gate of the pen open. When she came home from school, the pen was empty. Both Herman and the calf had disappeared. Cindy looked all over the barnyard, behind the stable and all around the stable and the corncrib but there was no sign of the duck and the little blind calf.

Thinking that Herman might have gone for a swim, she followed the path through the woods down to the pond. There he was with some other ducks merrily swimming around and ducking his head under the water looking for snails or small fish to eat. He looked so funny when he dived down with only the tip of his tail showing!

Cindy looked around for Tiny Tim; then she saw him lying in the shade of a tree evidently taking his afternoon nap.

For fifteen minutes or so, Cindy sat there watching the ducks swimming about and diving for food. Then they began to swim for shore. Following their leader, they slowly walked in single file up the path that led through the woods. Cindy wondered if Tiny Tim would follow their squawking but he only raised his head and didn't make another move. However, when Herman waddled up the bank of the pond, and began his cheerful squawk, he immediately got to his feet and followed him up the path.

Cindy laughed gleefully and jumped up and down with excitement. "He knows the sound of Herman's squawk!" she exclaimed. "Herman, you really are a seeing-eye duck!"

Once, just as the duck turned his head, Tiny Tim stumbled against a tree. Herman let out a loud squawk as if to say, "Hey! Watch out! Why don't you stay close to me and listen to my squawk!"

Cindy followed them along the path through the woods and into the barnyard and, in a few minutes, Herman led Tiny Tim back to his pen.

The news about the little blind calf and the seeing-eye duck soon spread throughout the neighborhood. Almost every day someone stopped by to watch the duck waddling around the barnyard heading for the pond with Tiny Tim trudging behind. Herman had become the most famous duck in the whole countryside.

A St. Bernard Dog's Famous Rescue

In a park in Paris, stands a monument of a St. Bernard dog with a boy on his back. It commemorates the famous rescue of a boy who was buried under a snow slide in southern Switzerland. The dog found the boy asleep, buried under the snow.

Rex licked the boy's face to awaken him. When he saw the dog crouched over him, the boy threw his arms around the dog's neck and the dog started to drag him through the snow. Finally, the boy climbed up on the dog's back and the dog, barking loudly, attracted the attention of a searching party, and the boy's life was saved. It is said to be the most famous rescue by any St. Bernard dog. This beautiful St. Bernard has saved the lives of forty-one people who have been buried under the snow in the mountain country of Southern Switzerland.

The way these remarkable dogs have rescued people lost in the snow is a thrilling story. They are trained at the St. Bernard hospice in southern Switzerland. One of the methods used by these monks at the hospice is to send the dogs out to rescue someone reported lost in the snow.

It's amazing how these dogs have the sense of smell to find someone even if he is covered with snow. When found, the dogs dig away the snow. Two of them are trained to lie down on either side and close to the helpless one to keep him warm, while the other dog, barking loudly, runs to his trainer and leads him back to the one who is in need of help.

The individual is then carried by dog sled to the hospice where he is warmed and given food to help his recovery.

What a wonderful instinct God has given these dogs that they can do what a human being can't do—find a

TRUE TALES To Live By

person who is lost in the snow covered mountains of Switzerland.

The Loving Bull Moose

One of the things which was quite obvious at the exotic animal auction we attended recently in South Dakota was the love of many of the owners for the animals which they had brought to the sale. For them, the auction was not a happy experience, but a sad one. A cowboy had put on the auction block a cowpony he had used for years in rounding up cattle. One can imagine how sad he was at parting with the horse which had been his loyal friend for years.

A most touching incident happened one day at the sale barn when a big bull moose was scheduled to be sold. There was some delay in getting the bidding started, for the animal was so big he couldn't quite get through the door. The huge antlers seemed to be the main problem. The two auctioneers in the arena headed for the protective bars where they could feel safe from those wicked looking antlers. They knew a bull moose could be very dangerous.

However, the owner of the animal seemed to have no fear. He stood in front of the moose and pulled down on his horns until finally the animal was able to get into the arena. The incident was great fun for the spectators who burst into laughter at the desperate efforts of the owner to get his animal through the door. The moose was a beautiful specimen of an animal with its brownish black upper coat and the growth of skin covered with hair, called *the bell*, which hung beneath its throat. It stood seven feet high at the shoulder and weighed fifteen hundred pounds. The antlers had a spread of about six feet. Each antler had eight or ten short points, which stuck out like fingers from a hand.

One of the auctioneers ventured from behind the barred cage for a moment but quickly retreated to safety as the moose lunged at him with his wide spreading antlers.

The owner stood quietly in the center of the arena, waiting for the bidding to begin. For a moment the moose stood looking curiously at the crowd of spectators; then he slowly walked over to his master who reached into a pouch at his side and offered the moose a sandwich.

"This is his favorite food," he announced. "Ham sandwiches."

After the owner had emptied his bag of the ham sandwiches, he signaled the auctioneer to begin the bidding. The sad look on his face indicated he wasn't very eager to part with that moose. His friends knew he had raised the animal from a calf and that he was parting with him only because he needed the money. As the auctioneer's chant rang through the sale barn, the bidding began. There were several in the audience who wanted that moose.

As the owner gently stroked the neck of his pet, the animal reached over and rubbed his nose on the man's shoulder; then to the amusement of the spectators, the moose kissed him on the cheek. Those sitting nearby could see a trace of tears in the man's eyes at this gesture of affection. The auctioneer paused for a moment, then raised his voice to continue his chant. Suddenly the owner raised his hand to interrupt him.

"I'm sorry," he announced, "but I can't sell this animal. I'm taking him back home."

With that he walked toward the exit with the moose following close behind. The crowd burst into applause. They were all lovers of animals and they were deeply moved by this man's affection for a wild animal and the moose's love for his master.

A Dog Finds a New Home

Charlie was an orphan. His parents and grandfather had died, and for several months he had been living with his grandmother.

TRUE TALES To Live By

She was a kindly old lady, and often left the house to help her neighbors, who were in trouble, leaving Charlie alone in the house.

It was lonely for Charlie in the big house at night. There was a shotgun behind the closet door, but he didn't know much about guns. Anyway, if a burglar broke into the house, what chance would a ten-year-old boy have facing an armed robber with a gun?

There had been reports about burglars breaking into houses in the neighborhood. Often Charlie thought, "I wish I had a dog...a police dog like the ones that ride in the cars with the police. Then I would feel safe at night."

When Charlie said his prayers that night before going to bed, he prayed, "Please God, help me get a dog. Grandma can't buy one." But day after day passed, and there was no answer to Charlie's prayer.

One night there was a report on the radio that robbers had broken into a house just a block up the street. If only Charlie had a dog to protect him on that dark, dreary night!

Suddenly there was a sound at the front door. First it was a thump, thump, and then it sounded like a scratch, as if someone was trying to pick the lock. He could call the police but how long would it take them to get to his house?

Trembling with fright, the boy hurried to the closet and quickly loaded the gun.

"If I could sneak around the house," Charlie thought, "I could shoot in the air and scare that man away."

Trying not to make any noise, the boy hurried to the back door; then he crept around the house and peered around the corner. He cocked the gun and was going to shoot over the roof of the back porch but in the dim porch light he saw the intruder. It was not a man but a dog! A big dog, it looked like a German Shepherd.

Lowering his gun, Charlie cautiously approached the dog and gently said, "Good dog! You're my friend, aren't you? Good dog!" Then he patted the animal on the head.

To Charlie's surprise, it greeted him with a lick on the face. Excitedly he fitted a key into the lock and let the dog into the house.

"I'll bet you're hungry," Charlie exclaimed, as he took a dish from the cupboard and filled it with milk which his new friend eagerly lapped up. Then Charlie took a couple of hot dogs from the refrigerator and the dog devoured them and looked at the boy with pleading eyes as if begging for more.

In his excitement, Charlie hadn't noticed that the dog stood on three legs. "Why you poor dog. You've been hurt," he exclaimed. "There's blood on that leg!"

"I wish Grandma were home," Charlie thought. "She could fix that leg."

Just then he heard the sound of steps on the porch. It was Grandmother!

"Grandma, look who came to see us," Charlie exclaimed excitedly. "I heard a scratching at the door and I thought it was a robber. I loaded the gun and crept around the house to scare him away. It was a dog scratching at the door, not a robber."

"Isn't he beautiful? He's a German Shepherd. See, he's black with brown feet and brown legs."

Grandmother knelt down beside the dog and stroked him gently.

"Yes, he is beautiful," she said, "but why did he come to our door?"

"That's the funny part of it," Charlie exclaimed. "I think he needed help. See, his one leg has blood on it."

The dog whimpered as Charlie touched the leg.

"Poor dog! He has been hurt," Grandmother exclaimed sympathetically. "Let's wash it with some soap and water. Please get me that tin dish from the cupboard and that jar of ointment."

Tenderly, Grandmother washed the wound, put on some healing ointment and carefully bandaged the wounded leg.

TRUE TALES To Live By

Charlie had trouble getting to sleep that night. The dog lay on a rug beside him. In his prayer, Charlie said, "Thank you, Lord, for answering my prayer. I'm sure you sent that dog, 'cause otherwise where did he come from and why did he scratch at our door? I once read about a police dog named Bart so that will be his name."

The next morning at the breakfast table, there was a discussion about what should be done about the dog.

"We can keep him, can't we, Grandma?" Charlie pleaded.

"No, son. His owner is probably sad because he didn't come home, and he doesn't belong to us."

Charlie didn't answer, but he had a lump in his throat, and he suddenly lost his appetite for breakfast.

The grandmother looked at him sympathetically. "I'd like to keep the dog but if there's no notice in the paper in a few days about a lost dog, we'll have to put an ad in the newspaper to try and find the owner."

Several days passed and Charlie and Bart were inseparable. The dog limped a bit at first, because of his bandaged leg, but soon learned to give a slight bark when he was asked to say, "Please" and he rolled over at the boy's command.

One day Grandmother greeted Charlie with the sad announcement that the newspaper carried an advertisement with the description of a lost dog that looked like Bart. The owner would appreciate it if anyone knowing of its whereabouts would notify him.

A telephone call was made to the owner and that night the doorbell rang. The man at the door announced that he lived on the other side of town, about two miles away, and couldn't understand why the dog had wandered so far from home.

It was a tearful young boy that said goodbye to the dog he had learned to love so much. The grandmother tried to comfort Charlie. She put her arms around him and said sympathetically, "I'm sorry, son. I loved Bart, too, but it was the only honest thing we could do."

That night Charlie sobbed into his pillow, "Dear God, you know what is best. That man probably loved Bart, too, but why did you send me that beautiful dog and then let that man take him away from me?"

Several days passed and Charlie tried to get accustomed to not having a dog around the house, although he missed Bart very much.

One evening, he and his grandmother were sitting by the table, reading, when they heard a scratching sound at the door. Charlie sat for a moment in wide-eyed amazement.

"Grandma," he exclaimed, "do you suppose...?"

Then jumping from his chair, which he knocked over in his excitement, he rushed to the door. He flung it open and who should be sitting there wagging his tail, but Bart!

Charlie threw his arms around the dog and wept for joy.

"Son," said the grandmother with tears in her eyes, "I know why you feel so happy, but don't be disappointed if Bart's owner comes back for him."

That evening Charlie and Bart had a great time playing together, but the boy feared that it wouldn't last for long.

Just about bedtime, the telephone rang. Charlie picked up the phone and was not surprised when the voice on the other end of the line asked, "Did my dog, by any chance, come back to your house?"

"Yes, Sir," Charlie answered haltingly, "he did come back tonight."

There was a moment of silence as Charlie thought, "I've lost him again!"

Then with a sigh the man answered, "If that dog is so determined to live with you, I guess we can't do anything about it. You can have him."

Needless to say, joy and thankfulness reigned in the house that night and for a long time thereafter. Bart was a lovable member of the family.

TRUE TALES To Live By

A Child Saved by an Elephant

The Wirth Circus was playing under the big top in Sydney, Australia. The show was half over and the grand parade was in progress. Suddenly, in the midst of the din and the sound of the circus band, came a woman's frightened scream, "My child! Someone save my child!"

Her little daughter, for some strange reason, had left her mother and run right into the path of elephants. These elephants were trained, but if some strange object should suddenly appear in their path, they were apt to become frightened and might trample it.

The mother feared that was about to happen, for suddenly one of the elephants in the front line started toward the little girl. The elephant picked the child up in her trunk and lifted her off the ground. The horrified spectators in the audience expected that the elephant would hurl the girl to the ground and trample the victim under her feet.

But she did no such thing. To the amazement of the thousands of people in the stands, the elephant slowly walked toward the mother; then she carefully deposited the child in the mother's arms. The spectators broke into wild applause. Most of them did not know that the animal that performed this unusual feat was the best known elephant in Australia. Her name was Alice and the newspapers had carried numerous stories about the amazing exploits of this famous performer in the Wirth's Circus.

On one occasion, she had saved the life of Eileen Wirth, a member of the circus family. One of the circus elephants had rushed at Eileen and had knocked her to the ground with her trunk. She was about to stomp on her when Alice ran over and gave the attacking elephant a mighty butt with her head. Her quick action saved the girl from a horrible death.

It was well known that Alice loved children. One day when the circus tent had been set up in a West Australian park, Alice and her trainer were watching two small boys playing on a seesaw. One of the boys decided to leave. The other boy sat for a few moments looking at the elephant. To his surprise, the animal decided that she wanted to get in on the fun. Ambling over, she gently put one foot on the empty end of the board and slowly pressed it down. She watched the boy go up; then lifted her foot to let him down. This was so much fun that she continued at the game for several minutes, to the delight of her companion. That boy is undoubtedly the only boy who has ever played teeter-totter with an elephant.

The story of the loveable Alice shows us how some animals who were formerly wild have a deep love for people. God has created many animals, not only for our entertainment, but also for our protection.

The Tramp and the Little Black Dog

It was a cold winter's day in the snow-covered countryside east of Springfield, Illinois. A tramp, walking along the railroad tracks, was accompanied by his constant companion, a little black dog. Suddenly, the tramp heard a train whistle. As the train approached, the tramp noticed that it was traveling quite slowly, and the thought occurred to him that he might jump it and catch a ride to the next town.

Holding Blackie firmly under his arm, he waited at the crossing until the engine had passed, then he leaped for the ladder of one of the freight cars. As he jumped, his foot slipped and he was struck by the wheels of the moving train. When he fell, his dog leaped from his master's arms and escaped unharmed.

As the tramp lay beside the track, the dog licked his face and whined piteously, unable to understand why he lay there so still without speaking to him. As the train was disappearing in the distance, a farmer and his wife came driving down the road in their truck. Seeing the man lying beside the railroad tracks, they ran over to investigate.

The farmer, who had often seen the tramp in a neighboring town, exclaimed, "Oh no! It's Old Willie! I'm afraid he's done for. He has jumped his last train!"

Hurrying back to his car, he drove to the nearest farmhouse and called for an ambulance. When he returned to the scene, his wife made a suggestion.

"Let's take the dog home with us," she said. "He looks so sad and forlorn. He must have really loved poor Old Willie."

"That's a good idea," her husband replied. "Blackie will be lost without old Willie. He traveled with him wherever he went. Come here, Blackie. You come with us. We'll give you a good home."

After the ambulance had taken Old Willie away, the farmer and his wife returned home and offered the little dog some food, but in spite of much coaxing, Blackie refused to eat a bite. Finally, his new master put the dog in a shed, closed the door and left for the fields.

When he came home from work that night, he was greeted by his wife with the news that Blackie was gone.

"That little dog somehow got the door open," she said sadly. "He has disappeared."

They immediately drove over to the railroad crossing where the accident had happened and, just as they thought, there was Blackie with his chin on his paws near the spot where he had last seen his beloved master.

Once more they took him home, but the dog only nibbled at the food and soon disappeared again.

"What are we going to do?" the man asked of his wife. "The poor little fella will starve if we can't get him to eat."

"Why don't you take some food to him by the railroad crossing. That's probably where he is now," his wife suggested.

So they took some meat and other scraps from the breakfast table and drove over to the crossing. There he was and this time he ate greedily.

For several days after that, either the farmer or his wife carried food to Blackie, but whenever they took him home, he always refused to eat.

One morning the farmer said to his wife, "We can't let that little dog stay out there without shelter when the rains come and it turns colder. Let's build a house for him right on the spot."

They did just that. They built a little house for Blackie with the help of children in the neighborhood who had heard the sad story of Old Willie and Blackie.

Soon the boys and girls who lived nearby began to take turns bringing Blackie food. Always he greeted them with a wag of his tail as if to say thank you for the kindness. The children made sure that not a day passed without someone bringing the little dog something to eat and seeing that there was fresh water for his water dish.

This went on for many months, until one morning when they arrived to bring Blackie his food, they were saddened to see that the little dog was dead. The word spread throughout the countryside. Farmers came in from their fields and the children who had brought Blackie food came to mourn his passing.

As they stood together by his graveside, someone said a prayer of remembrance for Old Willie and recalled how he wandered from place to place. There was probably no one in the world who loved him but little Blackie.

Then it was suggested that a monument be placed there in memory of Old Willie and his dog.

If you drive by that railroad crossing today, you will see a stone figure of a little black dog and engraved below it, the word, "Blackie."

What a beautiful thing love is, even if it's only the devotion of a little dog for his master.

A bus driver told this story to me as I traveled on a highway east of Springfield, Illinois. He pointed out the monument as we passed by that railroad crossing.

TRUE TALES To Live By

Buster and the Angry Bull

It was milking time and an Iowa farmer, Hugo Swalin, was out in the pasture bringing in the cows.

"Come Boss, come Boss," he called out, but the cows were enjoying the lush green grass and weren't ready to come home.

As he circled around behind them to drive them to the barnyard, his dog, Buster, who was following along behind, gave a loud bark. Hugo turned around to see what was disturbing the dog. He saw why Buster was barking. He was warning Hugo about a bull that was slowly sneaking up behind him.

Hugo stopped and faced the bull; then the bull stopped and began to paw the ground. Hugo was so frightened that he stood still, rooted to the spot. He knew that he couldn't outrun that bull. Suddenly, there flashed through his mind what had happened to a neighbor. One day when he was out in the pasture bringing in the cows, an angry bull had charged the neighbor and trampled him to death.

"Dear God," Hugo prayed. "I need help. Please stop that bull!"

Suddenly the bull lowered his head and charged. At that moment, Hugo's prayer was answered. With a loud bark, Buster leaped at the bull and with an angry snarl tore at his flank with his sharp teeth. The bull turned and headed for the dog, but Buster was too quick for him. Several times, the bull charged at Buster but each time the dog got out of his way.

"Get him, Buster," Hugo shouted. "Go get him boy!"

Finally the bull became exhausted, and probably very frustrated. He turned and slowly trotted back toward the barnyard, like a dog with his tail between his legs. Buster followed behind him, now and then, nipping at his heels.

Hugo was so weak with fright that he forgot all about the cows and headed back toward the house.

SKIP WESTPHAL

As he came up the walk, his wife who was standing at the door exclaimed, "Hugo! Are you all right? You're pale as a ghost!"

"I'm alright," Hugo replied in a shaky voice as he slumped down on the back steps, "but I've just had an awful scare." Then he told her how good old Buster had saved him from the attack by the bull.

Hugo's wife put her arms around him and thanked the Lord for saving her husband from a terrible tragedy. Then she hugged Buster, too, for what he had done in that scary situation.

"What I don't understand," she said in a puzzled tone of voice, "is why Buster went out with you to get the cows. He has never gone out with you in the pasture. How did he happen to be with you today?"

"That puzzles me, too," Hugo replied. "He always follows me around when I'm doing chores and when I'm with the cows in the barnyard, but he never goes with me when I go to the pasture."

Then after a moments' pause, he added, "Vivian, Buster must have sensed that the bull was in a bad mood today, and he went along to protect me. I know this, we're going to get rid of that bull!"

Whenever Hugo told the story about his frightening experience with the angry bull, everyone marveled at how the dog could have sensed that on this particular day, he must go along to bring in the cows because he sensed that his master was going to be in danger. To that Iowa farmer, there was no doubt in his mind but that the Lord had led his faithful dog to save him from certain death. Hugo Swalin is a neighbor of mine and told me this amazing story.

TRUE TALES To Live By

The Tiger and the Puppy

One winter, the people in a village in northern Korea were filled with fear by the appearance of a huge tiger. No one had ever seen one as big as this. One night a man ventured out into the street after dark. He was attacked by the tiger. It carried him away and he was never seen again.

So many cows and pigs became victims of this ferocious beast that the people of the village decided they would set traps for him. They dug huge pits at the ends of the streets and covered them with branches that were overlaid with dirt and leaves. But the tiger was too clever for that. He stayed away from the traps, and the cows and pigs continued to disappear.

Finally the villagers decided that they would organize a hunting party from the entire surrounding countryside. They gathered together a small army of brave and experienced hunters. All day long the hunters searched for the tiger through the wooded hills but they returned at night empty-handed. They hadn't even gotten a glimpse of the *Mountain Uncle*.

The failure of the hunters to kill the tiger deepened the fear in the hearts of the people. At night, they locked up their animals in the barns, and no one dared to venture out on the street after darkness had fallen.

One cold winter's night, the yellow and black beast came prowling down the village street, looking for prey. For several nights all of the animals had been securely locked in their stables and the tiger was very hungry. He would have been satisfied with even a dog for an evening meal but the dogs were out of sight, too, except for one foolish little puppy that had strayed away from its mother and was poking his head through the tiny door in the gate. The tiger saw the little dog peering through the hole and with an angry snarl he leaped at him. But the puppy darted back and the hole was too small for the huge tiger to get through.

The tiger was so hungry he decided that he would try to leap the wall to get his prey. It was a high wall with jagged rocks at the top but with one mighty effort, the beast cleared the wall and leaped into the courtyard. Imagine his disappointment when he got only a glimpse of the puppy's tail as he disappeared through the hole out into the street.

Snarling with rage and disappointment, the beast scrambled back over the wall in pursuit of the puppy. But when the puppy saw the form of the tiger appearing at the top of the wall, he quickly scurried back through the hole into the safety of the courtyard.

Now that tiger was not only hungry, but he was also stubborn, as all tigers are, and he was determined to get the elusive puppy. Again and again he leaped over the wall as the smart little puppy crawled back and forth through the hole in the gate.

The next morning when the people of the village went out into the street, they found the tiger lying dead. His heart had given out from jumping over the wall in pursuit of the puppy. In the hole in the gate they found the little puppy fast asleep.

TRUE TALES To Live By

A Dolphin to the Rescue

> *Courteously he'll come—nudge me with his beak or take my foot into his mouth saying, 'I love you,' then like the wind under the water go to his own encounters.*
>
> —Margaret Bingham

That is how a poet and lover of dolphins expresses her affection for dolphins, these magical creatures of the deep. Ever since I stood on my balcony overlooking the Gulf of Mexico and was entertained by the antics of these joyous creatures as they leaped and dived gracefully above the waves, I have been entranced by the study of their habits. Time and again I have heard stories of their love for people and their dislike for sharks.

In his book entitled, *The Dolphin—Cousin to Man*, Robert Stenuit makes the following statement: "A dolphin could kill a man with a blow of his snout. It could dismember him with a blow of his jaws, because it possesses a double row of strong conical teeth, 80 in all, which sink in with precision. But never, absolutely never, has a dolphin or a porpoise attacked a man, even in legitimate defense, or with a harpoon in his side when it has been massacred in the name of science."

I once read a story of a man who was having a playful swim with a dolphin when the creature gently took the swimmers leg in his mouth. He knew that in seconds, the dolphin could have crushed the leg with its teeth but it did him no harm.

A fisherman's boat caught fire and he was forced to leap into the water infested by sharks. Those sharks were driven away by dolphins. According to the story, a dolphin pressed his snout against the man's back and pushed him to shore.

I could believe the account of how the dolphins had attacked the sharks but it was difficult for me to accept the description of the dolphin as having enough intelligence to actually push the man to shore.

Natural History magazine describes the experience of the wife of a well-known Florida attorney. While swimming, she was caught by a terrific undertow that began to pull her away from the shore. Gasping for breath, she prayed, "Please God, can't someone push me ashore!" With that, she reported, "someone gave me a tremendous shove and I landed on the beach, face down and too exhausted to turn over."

When she opened her eyes, no one was near, but in the water about twenty feet out, a dolphin was leaping around. A friend who had witnessed the incident from a distance said a dolphin had pushed the swimmer ashore, and it was his belief it was trying to protect her from a fishtail shark.

She concluded her story with the words, "God certainly was with me!"

I was convinced these stories were true when I met Dick Wachter, a resident of our condominium.

During World War II, Dick served in the navy at the U.S. Naval Air Training Station, Barin Field, Alabama, which was located on the Gulf of Mexico. He told how that area over the Gulf of Mexico was swarming with airplanes, some of them on training missions, others on the lookout for German submarines that prowled along the West Coast of Florida. Occasionally there were collisions in the air that forced the crew to parachute into the gulf waters, which were infested with sharks.

He said he heard several navy flyers report that on plunging into the water, they were attacked by sharks and were saved by dolphins that drove away the sharks and pushed the sailors to shore. These stories convinced me that the reports were indeed true of the remarkable way in which these creatures of the sea have come to the rescue of human beings who faced a horrible death from attacks by sharks.

TRUE TALES To Live By

A Strange Dog Was her Protector

A teenage girl had gone to Philadelphia looking for work. Her finances were limited, so she rented a room in a tenement house, which she soon learned was in a rather undesirable area. Almost every night there were reports of stabbings and muggings.

She succeeded in getting a position in an office that made it necessary for her to travel by subway to within about two blocks of her room. As she climbed the stairs at the subway exit at the end of her first day's work, she dreaded the thought of her two-block walk to the tenement house where she lived. When she reached the top of the stairs, she glanced nervously up and down the street and was uneasy at the sight of several—obviously drunken—men standing at the street corner.

"Oh dear!" she thought, "will I be able to make it to my room without being accosted by one of these disreputable looking characters?"

The words of the psalmist, "The angel of the Lord campeth about them that fear Him" flashed through her mind, and just then a big St. Bernard dog appeared among the pedestrians and stood beside her. She was puzzled because she knew that stray dogs were not allowed in the city.

She glanced down at the dog for a moment, then in a surprised tone of voice she said, "Aren't you a bit mixed up, you beautiful dog. You must be looking for someone else."

The dog looked up at her with a friendly wag of his tail and when the light changed and she started across the street, he walked beside her.

The girl was puzzled but very grateful for her new friend's protection. She knew that she was perfectly safe as she walked down the street with that big dog beside her.

When she reached the door of her flat, she gave the dog a pat on the head and said, "Thank you, Bernie, for your

34

protection. Wait here just a minute and I'll see if I can get a treat for you."

Climbing up the creaky stairs, she opened the door of her room, went to the refrigerator and returned with a wiener for the dog that was waiting patiently outside the door for her to return. She gave him the treat that he gratefully received; then he disappeared down the street.

The following day when the girl returned from work, she wondered if that big St. Bernard would be at the subway exit. He was there, standing patiently, waiting for her. The girl was overwhelmed at the protection which she was convinced the Lord had provided for her. Each day the dog walked faithfully beside her until she reached the door of her tenement and each day she gave him a treat before he disappeared into the night.

At the end of the week, she was able to arrange for a room nearer her work in a better part of the city. On Monday, as she left the office and entered the subway, she wondered if her faithful dog would be waiting for her like he had for several days. Then she thought, "If that dog was sent by my guardian angel to protect me, he won't be waiting for me today." Now she felt safe walking down the street.

She was right. The dog wasn't there to greet her when she left the subway exit.

From that day on, she related to her friends and acquaintances the amazing story about that St. Bernard dog. Some of them were a bit dubious about it and wondered if she had made up the story, but others believed her tale and thanked the Lord for the beautiful miracle He had wrought in her life.

TRUE TALES To Live By

A Mule Saved his Life

One day recently I had an appointment with my optometrist, Dr. Kolesar. I always enjoy these sessions with him. He is a lover of wild life and an expert photographer. He often has an unusual story to tell about the birds and animals that inhabit an area where he lives. He told me about an unusual pet that comes to visit their home. It is a wild turkey. She leaves the flock in the spring and rejoins it in September. Usually in the morning it appears at the door for a treat of several handfuls of shelled corn the doctor throws to it. The Kolesars can't get closer to that turkey than a few feet, but there is something that leads that turkey to spend the summer months in the friendly atmosphere of that country home.

Another incident that Dr. Kolesar and I have in common is that his father and my father both immigrated from the *old country* on a cattle boat. The difference was that my father came from Germany at the age of eight months while Dr. Kolesar's father, John Sr., was fourteen years old when he landed in America. What courage that must have taken for a fourteen-year-old boy, unable to speak or understand a word of English, to come alone over the ocean to a strange country!

We don't know much about Dr. Kolesar's father the next few years, except that he finally arrived in Fort Dodge, Iowa, and obtained work in the gypsum mines. In those days, the mining was done underground. There was no surface mining as there is today.

In the mining procedure, the miner went down into a mine with a mule hitched to a cart on which gypsum was loaded. It was a very dangerous occupation as there were frequent cave-ins of which the miner was not aware until it was too late.

The miner often unhitched the mule from the cart when he entered the mine. If there should be a sudden break-through, and the cart was loaded, it would take longer for the mule to pull out the cart to safety. The amazing characteristic of the mule is that he is aware of a breakthrough before the miner suspects it. He gives the warning by laying his ears back and braying loudly.

This sense of a threatening danger is true of other animals as well. I have heard that cats are often nervous and disturbed before an earthquake is predicted.

One day, John and his mule, Jack, had entered the mine and the cart was almost loaded when the mule suddenly put back his ears and started to bray loudly.

John dropped his pick, grabbed his mule by the tail and they escaped from the mine as a wall caved in. In seconds, it would have killed both the miner and his mule.

One can imagine how grateful that miner was to his mule. They both would have been crushed if the mule had not given his warning. I am sure, from that time on, John kept an eye on his mule while he was digging out the gypsum so he could be aware if Jack sensed there was danger of a cave-in.

This was not the only time that John faced danger and his mule saved him. He later told his family that five times his mule had saved his life. I'm sure that John Kolesar had many a time put his arm around Jack's neck and thanked him for his rescue.

My dad once owned a team of mules. I never had the affection for them that I did for horses. They have a reputation for being very stubborn.

But after hearing this amazing tale about Jack, I have a new respect for the mule. If I had lived in that time, I would not only have had respect for his mule; I would have loved him.

TRUE TALES To Live By

Under the Big Top

I n my true tales about God's creatures I must include my love for horses. As a boy on an Iowa farm, we did all of our fieldwork with horses.

There was one mare named Daisy. When she died, she was buried in the grove back of the barn and many a tear was shed over her grave.

It was my love for horses that led me into one of the most exciting adventures of my life. While on a business trip to Florida, I visited the winter quarters of the Ringling Brothers and Barnum and Bailey Circus in Sarasota, Florida. All the sights were wonderful to behold but I was particularly interested in the horses. In two large stables were almost a hundred beautiful Kentucky bred sorrels. Then there were the clumsy looking Percherons used in the bareback riding acts. The loveable little Shetland ponies and the graceful, white, dancing horses were especially intriguing.

Suddenly it occurred to me that here was my opportunity to live again some of my boyhood experiences with horses. Why not put my business on the shelf for a while and join the circus! I was selling my own line of stationery to gift shops in Florida and was responsible only to myself.

I must confess it was not an entirely new idea. As a boy I used to long to join the circus. I decided to give it a try.

It wasn't too easy realizing my dream. For two weeks, day after day, I drove over to the circus grounds and talked with Indian Joe, the head of the ring stock. Finally I made it.

The first day wasn't quite what I had anticipated. These high-spirited show horses were different from our gentle farm horses. I didn't feel exactly comfortable when I was told that one of the horses assigned to me had kicked a groom in the chest the previous year and put him in the hospital for three months.

SKIP WESTPHAL

Skip holding the head of Abraham Lincoln preceding the big parade.

I gulped a bit when I learned that another one, named Night Rider, would do his best to crush his keeper against the partition or to sink his teeth into one's arm at the first opportunity.

One of my first jobs was a rough and tumble experience. I was told to lead two black carriage horses around the stable yard. They had come in from a strenuous run and had to be walked for awhile so they wouldn't cool off too quickly and catch cold.

The horses seemed to sense that an inexperienced hand had them by the bit, for they started rearing up in an effort to break away. One of them, a mean looking black gelding, would rear up and strike out with his front feet in a terrifying manner. With the horse on the left pulling in the opposite direction, you can see it wasn't an easy matter to keep from being struck by one of those big front feet.

Around and around the stable yard we went. I was hanging on for dear life, praying that someone would come and lend me a hand. The horses were dragging me dangerously near to the watering trough. That worried me. I knew that a horse would founder if he drinks when he's too hot. If those horses ever got to the water in their heated condition, it might mean that two valuable show horses might be ruined. Then what would become of the amateur circus man? I shuddered to contemplate it!

At last help came! With the horses only a couple feet from the watering trough, I was about to collapse, when one of the grooms returning from supper saw my predicament and took over.

As I dragged my weary bones to the cookhouse that night, my idea of being a part of the *greatest show on earth* seemed a bit dim. Maybe that business of mine really needed attention!

The next day was easier. I was beginning to learn something about the technique of handling high-strung show horses. When the horses I was leading seemed on the verge of rearing up, I'd remember the advice of the stable boy. "Keep their heads together! Push your elbows against their shoulders. When they lower their heads, as they always do before rearing up, throw your whole weight on the bits." It worked! The horses began to sense that they could no longer scare the wits out of me.

The feeling I had the night before that these horses had mean dispositions was somewhat changed by a remark of one of the grooms. "That horse," he said, "isn't trying to be mean when he rears up and strikes with his front feet. He's just trying to have a little fun!"

Give Her a Lot of Propaganda

My next job was that of cleaning out the hoofs of forty horses used in the Liberty Act. This had to be done to prevent a foot infection known as *thrush*. All the dirt had to be dug out with a hoof-hook and the inside of the hoof washed out with soap and water. Picking up the front hoofs was easy, but to walk into a stall with a strange horse with the reputation of being a kicker and pick up his hind foot, wasn't exactly my idea of fun. Luckily, I got through the ordeal without any serious mishaps.

The experienced horseman in this kind of situation knows the importance of talking reassuringly to the horse to keep him calm. The groom who was holding the hoof as I cleaned it would keep admonishing me to speak to the horse.

"Talk to her," he would say. "Give her a lot of propaganda! Tell her how nice she is!"

The moment I stopped talking, he'd call out, "Speak to her! Speak to her! Give her some propaganda!"

So I'd pet the horse and keep repeating, "Good girl! That's a good girl! Take it easy now. That's a good girl!"

It was amazing to see how a few soft words would calm a nervous horse. The wild gleam in her eyes would disappear. She would look at me in a trusting sort of way, and make no more objections to the cleaning up process.

The friendly groom stopped once in his work to make a philosophical reflection.

"Handling horses," he said, "is like getting along with women. A few soft words will accomplish a lot. Tell a lady how wonderful she is and how much you think of her and you'll soon have her eating out of your hand! The same thing is true of horses."

Something like Teaching School

He was right—at least as far as those horses were concerned. But there are times with some horses when a good firm word gets better results. The head veterinary, Doc Henderson, told me one day how he had just started to enter a stall when the horse put back his ears and raised one hind leg to kick.

"Prince!" he called out in a commanding tone. "Put it down!"

TRUE TALES To Live By

Prince stood there a moment on his three legs with the other one raised ready to kick. He was looking squarely at Doc to see if he meant it. Then with a sheepish look, Prince slowly put the foot down. He decided that it was in his best interests not to kick after all. Doc chuckled as he recalled how ludicrous the horse looked standing on three legs and making up his mind whether to kick or not to kick.

Other horsemen, like Curley Brideson, knew instinctively when to speak soothingly and when to bark out in commanding tones. Curley had magic in his voice, which seemed to have a hypnotizing effect on the horses. This was partly due to the fact that he loved them, and they knew it. He loved them all, even the vicious problem children.

We Take to the Road

During my first weeks with the circus, the winter quarters at Sarasota were the scene of excitement and activity, with daily rehearsals for the big show. Beautiful horses were waltzing about in the arena, keeping time to the music of the band. Elephants were standing on their heads. Excited chimpanzees and barking dogs, acting like cowboys, were riding ponies all over the place. Under the big top the trapeze performers were "flying through the air with the greatest of ease." Acrobats were doing somersaults and the clowns were rehearsing their funny capers.

When the time came for the show to take to the road, there was a big family of fourteen hundred people, over one hundred horses, twenty-nine elephants, and numerous wild animals. There were one hundred cars on the circus train headed for New York.

Farmers in the fields stopped work to gaze at the show train passing by. Women and children standing in the doors of their homes waved and cheered.

Two days and two nights, our big circus family spent en route. Finally we arrived in New York for the opening of the show. The cars were pulled on a siding in the train yards at the outskirts of the city. That meant a horseback ride of about nine miles through the city traffic to Madison Square Garden. Each man in ring stock rode a horse, bareback, and led two. I never dreamed that one day I would be riding a horse and leading two others down Broadway in the midst of the noisy city traffic as a part of a circus procession behind a herd of elephants.

Some Strange Bedfellows

When we arrived at the Garden, all the animals, including the elephants, lions, and tigers, were kept together in the basement. The men in ring stock slept near their horses. These men made their beds in the straw, or on bales of hay.

The noise and commotion that first night was nothing short of bedlam. In my quiet life as a teacher and a writer, I never dreamed that the time would come when I'd have trouble getting to sleep because of roaring lions, trumpeting elephants, and braying donkeys! I might almost as well have been in the heart of a jungle instead of one block off Broadway!

Most of my time was spent taking care of the three gray Percherons used in one of the bareback riding acts. They looked like big, clumsy plow horses but they were much gentler than the high-strung, prancing sorrels used in the Liberty Act. Their names were Champion, Blanca, and Hippo. Three more affectionate horses I have never known. They had a way of nibbling at my sleeve or the back of my shirt, when they wanted a lump of sugar. You can be sure that they always got it.

I have seldom had any pets to which I've been more devoted than to my three beautiful Percherons. My friendship with Champion, Blanca, and Hippo was one of the highlights of my circus experience.

TRUE TALES To Live By

When Dreams Come True

From New York the show moved to Boston. Of all my interesting experiences with *the greatest show on earth*, the biggest thrill came in Boston when I realized a lifelong ambition to ride a white horse in a circus parade. Dressed as a rebel soldier, I rode in the pageant, or *spec*, as it is called, along with Abraham Lincoln, George Washington, Teddy Roosevelt, and other historical characters.

The act's title, "When Dreams Come True," was certainly appropriate for me. This superbly costumed extravaganza, with its decorated floats and beautiful horses, was one of the most magnificent in circus history. It was an experience of a lifetime to be a part of it on my beautiful, prancing White Flash.

Later at Baltimore, an acrobat who had ridden in the parade as Abraham Lincoln quit the show and I was given his part. What a promotion, from a rebel soldier to president of the United States!

As I sat astride my horse, I wore a swallowtail coat, a tall silk hat and a mask which made me look like Abraham Lincoln. When my horse entered the arena, the circus band struck up "The Battle Hymn of the Republic," and, as instructed, I tipped my hat to the cheering crowd. That was an experience of a lifetime.

Leaving Old Circus Friends

After three exciting months under the big top, the day came when I had to lay aside the frock coat and tall silk hat. It was with regret that I turned in my resignation as president of the United States pro tem and said goodbye to my roustabout friends...and to Champion, Blanca, and Hippo. Bidding farewell to those three horses was almost like taking leave of Old Daisy when I was a kid back on the farm in Iowa.

But saying goodbye to Curley Brideson, the ring stock boss who had befriended me from my first day with the circus, really brought a lump to my throat. The evening show was almost over. Curley was leaning against a circus wagon when I approached.

"What's up, son?" he called out. "You look like you've lost your best friend!"

"I feel as if I have, Curley," I said. "You know, I'm going to leave you tonight."

"No!" he cried. "Don't tell me that you're leaving the show! I hate to see you do that! Wait until after tonight's performance and we'll talk it over."

But I felt there was no point in delaying my departure any longer. The time had come for me to go and get back to my former job.

There were tears in the eyes of the hardened old circus veteran as he put out his hand to wish me good luck.

As I hurried across the show grounds, I could hear the band blaring forth the accompaniment to the Grand Finale and the lights of the Big Top beckoned me to stay.

But I knew that if I didn't leave soon, instead of getting the circus fever out of my system, I'd get it into my blood.

I look back now on those rough and tumble thrilling days as one of the most worthwhile experiences of my life. I shall always cherish my memories of the sawdust ring and the Big Top. It's a good feeling to have that kind of childhood dream come true.

PIONEER DAYS

Trapped by a Prairie Fire

In writing tales about the early pioneer days, it is interesting to find that friends and neighbors tell some of the most unusual stories to me. They have remembered stories their parents or grandparents have told them about their experiences when life was simple but at times very difficult and even dangerous.

Such was the case one day when a neighbor, Earl Johnson, who lives a mile up the road from our home, dropped by for a visit. When he learned that I was interested in stories of pioneer days, he told me a tale he had heard about a country doctor who was returning from a call on a patient. His transportation was by a team of horses and a buggy. That was in the days when the doctors often drove many miles to minister to sick people who lived in sod houses or log cabins in the countryside.

The doctor's little daughter was traveling with him for company. She loved to be with her dad at every opportunity. The narrow road they were following led through a virgin prairie of tall grass almost as high as the top of their buggy. The little girl was enjoying the ride as she admired the beautiful wildflowers. There were sunflowers, goldenrod, goats' beard, daisies, black-eyed Susans, and many others that grew in abundance on both sides of the road.

Suddenly, the horses broke nervously into a fast trot, as if they sensed danger somewhere. The rabbits and ground squirrels scurried across the road as if they, too, were frightened by some unknown threat.

The father became suspicious and glanced to the north horizon where he noticed a bright glow lighting the sky. That meant a prairie fire was headed their way. If there had been a sod house in sight, they could have found refuge in it but their horses and buggy would have perished in the flames.

But there were no sod houses in sight and the wind was blowing so hard from the north and covering such a wide area that he knew the horses could not out run the fire. There was only one hope for them to escape the threatening flames.

Bringing his horses to a halt, the doctor leaped from the buggy and with his daughter's help they began frantically to gather bunches of grass into small piles on the south side of the road.

Hopefully, they could start a backfire, and with the help of the strong north wind could burn an island of grass south of the road. In that area, they could find safety from the flames that were approaching ever nearer.

Breathing a prayer for their safety, the father reached in his trouser pocket. With a sigh of relief, he found he had one match with which to start the fire. Nervously, he struck the match on the soul of his shoe. To his dismay, it failed to light. Now all hope was gone.

"Daddy," the frightened girl sobbed, "are we going to burn to death?"

Suddenly, she had an idea. Running to the buggy, she pulled a jacket from the seat.

"There's one match in the pocket of your coat!" she cried.

Excitedly, her father struck the match, and to his great relief it lit! Fanned by the wind, the fire spread to the south. In a few moments, it burned an area into which the doctor could drive his horses. Already they could feel the heat of the approaching fire.

Throwing a blanket over the horses' heads, he stood between them, and grasping their bits, he tried to quiet them while his daughter held onto his arm and prayed that God would save them from that horrible fire.

In a few moments, the flames roared around them. They had been saved by one match!

According to my neighbor's story, many years later when that girl became a mother and a grandmother she often related the story to her children and her grandchildren. She told of how she felt sad to see how the beautiful prairie had been reduced to miles and miles of black ashes.

She also told with a thankful heart how her father and she had been saved from death by one match!

Some Early Prairie Farmers Lived in Caves

When the pioneer settlers first arrived in the prairie country of the Midwest, there were few trees in some areas except those that grew near the riverbanks. As a result, log cabins were few in numbers. There is a town in Iowa named "Lone Tree" because only one tree could be seen for miles around.

Some prairie farmers created shelter from the rain and the cold by building sod houses. Others dug large holes in the side of a hill for their temporary homes. It doesn't seem possible that there was a time when a number of farmers in the vicinity of what is now Fort Dodge lived in caves. One of these caves was located two miles east of my home northwest of Manson.

Among the most amusing of the stories told to me by the relatives of these early settlers was about a family whose home was a cave in a hillside. The farmer had dug steps in the dirt leading down into the cave. The opening was covered with a blanket.

One rainy day a neighbor came to visit the *cave dweller*. He didn't realize how slippery those dirt steps were. Suddenly he found himself sliding down the steps into the cave. He landed underneath the table in the small room where the astonished housewife was preparing dinner. That incident was told and retold many times by those early pioneers who needed a good laugh now and then to lighten the burden of their rather primitive existence.

Another story told to me by a neighbor concerned a neighbor who lived with his family five miles northeast of Manson. He had walked into town to buy some groceries. As he was about to leave for home, a terrific blizzard suddenly struck the area and he feared he would get lost in the storm if he ventured out in it. For two days, he was unable to leave town due to the storm.

Finally the storm let up and he was able to travel, although the drifts across the road made walking difficult. When he reached the area where his wife and children were anxiously awaiting his return, he was unable to see the cave. Huge snowdrifts covered the place where he knew the cave existed.

He found a shovel and started digging in the snow banks. After almost an hour of feverish digging the distraught father located the cave. How relieved his wife and children were when the father rescued them. They were hungry, but none the worse for those days beneath that huge snowdrift.

The Strenuous Life of a Pioneer Homemaker

When we compare the home life of our present day to that of the pioneers, it's almost unbelievable. Here is a glimpse of the kind of life some of the homemakers had during these early pioneer days.

Today, when a housewife is planning meals, she finds the procedure for heating the food to be very simple. She simply places the pot or the dish on an electric or gas stove, and a turn of a knob is all that is required. If she prefers, there is the microwave oven that requires only a few seconds to press the buttons. With either method, the dish of food on the stove or in the microwave takes but a few minutes to prepare.

Now let us go back in our imagination to a pioneer wife in a sod house. Before she prepares the meals, she takes her wheelbarrow and starts out on the grassland surrounding her home in search of dried droppings—cow or buffalo chips. These hardened droppings were sometimes called the *coal of the plains*.

There were times when the mother would go barefooted in this rather unpleasant task. How long it would take the housewife to gather a heaping wheelbarrow full of the cow dung would vary.

If buffalo had recently roamed the area, or if the farmer owned several cattle, the task might be accomplished in less than an hour. Sometimes it would take longer. Gathering the chips would at first be a rather distasteful task. After a while the pioneer woman would become accustomed to it. It was a part of the day's work.

It is said that in her first experience of fueling the fire, the woman of the plains was very finicky about picking up the chips. She used two sticks, or a rag, or the corner of her apron; then she would wash her hands as she prepared the biscuits for the oven.

Some of the housewives would become careless about washing their hands and wouldn't bother to go through this procedure until they were ready to serve the meal. What a laborious, time consuming task some of our great-grandmothers had to endure to prepare meals for their families.

They spent most of their time growing and preparing food. The garden was often a half-acre in size. Vegetables were dried and stored for the winter. A large hole was dug in the ground and covered with boards. The vegetables were stored in the hole between layers of straw.

Washing the clothes was considered a chore by most of the women. Many of them had to carry buckets of water from nearby streams.

The next day was spent washing the clothes on a scrub board—a chore that took a great deal of energy. Since the washing took so much time and energy, all of the family members were expected to wear their clothes as long as possible. A common expression was "you wore the clothes until they were dirty enough to stand by themselves in a corner."

How long does it take today for a homemaker to do her washing? In about a minute's time, she can drop the dirty clothes in the washing machine; then go about her day. One minute to put the clothes in the washer as compared to almost two days for the pioneer wife to do her weekly washing.

Mending the clothes also took a great deal of time. One member of a very large family remembered that his mother didn't have time to keep all the clothes mended and once when the company was arriving, the boy and his brother were ordered to run into the woods and remain there until the company left.

Some of the sod houses were quite comfortable. Others had leaky roofs. A farmer who had lived in those early days says that he can remember when it was raining, he would hold an umbrella over the stove so his mother could cook without uninvited guests falling into the food. The uninvited guests were the bugs, grasshoppers and worms that had a way of getting into the sod house roof.

One might get the idea that life on the prairie would be very lonesome but women visited their neighbors, sometimes packing up their mending and their youngest children and staying the entire day. Women exchanged work with other women and this gave them a chance to visit as well. One of them would sew while a friend cared for her child. Life for Iowa's early families might have been difficult, but not lonely.

In those early days, there were many country churches that not only helped to meet the country folk's spiritual needs but enabled them to make friends as well.

Another problem for the family was the lack of the services of a doctor. It often required a trip of thirty or forty miles to reach a doctor. That was a long trip when the doctor could be reached only by horse drawn vehicles. Many times the parents had to serve as their own doctor. We find in reading the history of those early days that warm horse manure was a common remedy for rheumatism or other aches and pains. Urine was sometimes used for earache.

SKIP WESTPHAL

I remember when I was a small boy, my dad blew smoke from his pipe in my ear for earaches. I don't know whether that was a good remedy or not, but it seemed to work.

Traveling by Wagon Train

It is good for us who live in this world of gadgets and modern conveniences to reflect about those early pioneers who traveled by wagon train across the plains and over the mountains to new homes in the West.

It is interesting to note that some of those who traveled by wagon train in search of a new home left the southern states because they were unable to make a living without the help of slaves. Their conscience would not permit them to depend on slavery for their income.

These wagon trains often were a couple miles long and consisted of as many as one hundred wagons, each pulled by four oxen. In 1841, one of these journeys began at Independence, Missouri, and covered two thousand miles before these hardy travelers reached their destination. The beginning of the day had an air of excitement about it when a trumpeter blew a blast that was a signal for all of the travelers to be ready to start the day's journey.

For the most part, only a few—those who were ill or the very young—were permitted to ride in the wagons. The others had to walk most of the day. There wasn't much room in the wagons, for they were loaded with flour, bread, beans, bacon, dried fruit, coffee, feather beds, furniture and other supplies needed for the journey. There were few stores on the way where food could be purchased.

There were times when prairie fires were set by the Indians to impede the travelers progress, and enable the Indians to capture some of the travelers' livestock—cows, sheep and goats. These fires left nothing but ashes through which the men, women and children had to trod all day

TRUE TALES To Live By

long in a cloud of dust. Their faces would often be blackened by the soot by the end of the day. One wonders how they were able to take baths unless they were near a river.

Usually the pioneer travelers arranged their wagons in a huge circle at night, not only to better protect themselves from Indian attacks, but also to keep the milk cows, sheep and other livestock from wandering away.

Among these travelers were often talented musicians who were experts at playing the violin. This cheerful music would lift the spirits of the weary travelers and make the trials of the day more bearable.

One of the problems in these caravans was the rivers that had to be crossed. Often wagons were swept away on these crossings and livestock drowned. In the winter months, not only the snow, but also the cold rain, was a hazard. There were times when the water froze in the nostrils of the oxen at night and they died of suffocation.

Sometimes babies were born on the journey. A pregnant woman or a mother with a tiny baby riding all day in a bumpy wagon must have experienced quite an ordeal. Disease, too, was a serious problem. Typhoid fever, dysentery, tuberculosis, scarlet fever and malaria were diseases that often proved to be fatal.

The number of travelers who crossed the prairie, headed for the West Coast, is indicated by a record which was kept at Fort Laramie, Wyoming, in the year 1850. The record showed that, in one year, there passed that way, 7,472 mules, 30,616 oxen, 22,742 horses, 8,998 wagons, and 5,270 cows.

Many of these pioneers died before their destination was reached. On one stretch of a hundred miles, there was an average of five graves for every mile. There is a touching photograph that shows a small family group with arms about each other, mourning the death of a loved one. Even their pet dog sat there with head lifted, howling for the loss of his master.

Another sad event on the wagon trains was when the travelers ran short of food before the end of the journey and

SKIP WESTPHAL

were forced to slaughter some of their oxen to keep from starving to death. The oxen were not looked upon as mere beasts. Their owners were very fond of them and gave them names like Tom, Dick or Sam. So it was a sad experience to be forced to butcher them for food.

Do we feel sometimes that we have problems? Perhaps we would face our difficulties with a more cheerful spirit if we recalled what those brave pioneers endured in their search for a new home.

An Unexpected Visitor

What courage and endurance our early pioneers demonstrated! My neighbor Carl Steinbrink told me a story about his grandparents who immigrated to this country from Germany in those early pioneer days. His grandfather had served as bodyguard for Kaiser Wilhelm. The war clouds preceding World War I were hovering over Europe, and many were fleeing from the Kaiser's rule to safety in the United States.

On arriving in New York, the man and his wife traveled by train to Iowa Falls, Iowa. There the rail line ended. They found, to their dismay, that no transportation was available to Manson, sixty-five miles in the distance, as the crow flies. In those days if there was no ponds on the ice; then the distance would be even farther. They decided there was no choice but to walk the sixty-five miles to the home of relatives near Manson.

How those two hardy souls survived that long walk in the cold winter weather, and where they found shelter for the night, is not known. After that long hazardous journey, they had almost reached their relative's home when darkness fell and they could no longer see their way. To their great relief, a barn loomed up in the darkness, but there was no house in sight. They decided that they would have to make their bed for the night in the hayloft.

57

TRUE TALES To Live By

Just as they had burrowed down in the hay for warmth, they made a rather alarming discovery. They had thought their sleep might be disturbed by a visitor that cold winter's night, but this visitor was a surprise. The wife was pregnant, but she didn't think that the baby would decide this was the time for its entry into the world. Like the baby Jesus, the baby girl was born in a stable. Little Matilda didn't receive a very warm welcome into the world. She had a blanket to keep her warm, but it was a blanket of snow that had drifted through the roof on that cold winter's night.

What a joyous reception dad, mother, and baby received when they arrived at the home of their relatives the following day!

Soddies Provided Primitive Shelter

While passing through West Bend, Iowa, recently, I noticed an authentic sod house beside the road. I stopped to examine it and observed a sign that stated more than one hundred sod houses existed in Kossuth and Palo Alto counties at one time. Because of the fact that the walls and roofs were made of dirt, the little houses were in constant need of repair. One would think that a driving rain would soon *melt* the little house, but the grass and weeds growing on the sod no doubt helped to preserve it.

It reminded me of the story a neighbor related to me. His grandmother often told that when her father saw a glow on the horizon, he knew a prairie fire was sweeping their way. Their only refuge was their sod house where they would be safe from the roaring flames that swept around them. The grandmother told how frightening it was to hear the roaring of the fire all around them although they knew they would be safe in their dirt house.

Those pioneer families were very devout Christians. When they sang the old hymn, "The Lord's Our Rock, in

SKIP WESTPHAL

Him We Hide, a Shelter in the Time of Storm," they would think of their sod house and of how it had saved them from the dreaded flames of a prairie fire.

While the sod house was a refuge from prairie fires, it often was not too comfortable. Even today, we have problems similar to that of our ancestors when the electric power goes off.

One winter that happened in our home when the electricity was off for five days! Like our pioneer ancestors, we used a kerosene lamp to light the room, went to bed early with our family of five crawling under blankets near the fireplace to keep warm. We felt like pioneers living in a sod house for five days.

In a book, entitled *Iowa, Past to Present*, published by the Iowa State University Press, there is an interesting description of life in a pioneer log cabin.

> In Iowa, most early settlers built small log cabins that measured about sixteen feet. The cabins usually had one room with an overhead loft where the children slept during warm weather. When it turned cold, children slept on straw pallets in front of the fire.
>
> The fireplace was the chief feature in the cabin. In winter, it provided heat for the family and at night it gave light. Most important, the fireplace was the place for cooking food.
>
> Pioneer cabins were crowded. Most families had at least three or four children and everyone had to live in one or two rooms. With so many people, there was little space for furniture. Most cabins contained at least one bed, a small cupboard, a table, and a few chairs or stools. Pioneer women usually had a spinning wheel and a loom that they set up when they needed to weave cloth.
>
> During Iowa's cold winters, life was especially difficult. Often it was hard to stay warm. Sometimes in bitterly cold weather families went to bed

TRUE TALES To Live By

because that was the only way they could keep from getting badly chilled or even frostbitten. In the first years of settlement, some cabins did not have wooden floors, so the owners had to stand on the frozen ground. Sometimes pioneer women stood on a block of wood to do their work.

Dirt floors may be covered by preparing logs for a smooth surface. Split logs and hew the flat side with your broad axe. Place the logs side by side with the rounded side on the soil. The logs soon settle into the soil and you have a smooth walking surface. The floor is also warmer.

Families lived in soddies for years, discovering that the houses were cool in the summer and warm in the winter. Would the people who refer to *the good old days* like to go back to the sod houses and log cabins?

Traveling by Stage Coach

In these days of modern transportation, we can fly from Iowa to California in a few hours. How different was the means of travel for our grandfathers and great-grandfathers.

There was once a stagecoach line that ran from Fort Dodge, Iowa, to Sioux City, Iowa. The average speed a stagecoach traveled in those days was about four to five miles an hour. At that rate, it would take about two months to travel from Iowa to California.

On a stagecoach journey to Sioux City, there were times when the driver lost his way in the tall grass that was often as high as the wheels on his stagecoach. This was an especially frightening experience on a wintry day when there were biting northwest winds and the temperature was below zero. There were travelers who were lost in a blizzard out on the prairie, and the memory of that experience gave them nightmares for days afterwards. Some travelers froze to death on such a journey.

To avoid such a terrible fate, an engineer, Alexander McCready, made the western route safer by plowing two furrows in the prairie between Fort Dodge and Sioux City to guide the way.

The route the stages traveled was across snake infested sloughs, or around them, on the route to Sioux City. There was a stagecoach hotel at Twin Lakes. With our modern travel by bus and airplane, where restrooms are provided for the convenience of the travelers, one wonders how the restroom problem was taken care of on a stagecoach trip across the prairie.

An article in the Lake City Graphic, written by Eldon Watters, president of the Lake City Historical Society, describes an experience of the travelers when they arrived at the Williams Hotel in Lake City after an exhausting long day of travel from Fort Dodge.

"They were hungry and tired," he writes, "and about to be richly rewarded with a home-cooked meal of wild venison, mashed potatoes, rich gravy, parsnips, carrots, and homemade pumpkin pie covered with rich whipped cream. When time came to retire, they sank into a deep bed of feathers where they slept soundly until the early morning call to breakfast."

Certainly none of us desire to return to the old stagecoach days but when we read about the spread of crime and the threat of nuclear war, we wonder if we are really better off then were the pioneers of 150 years ago.

How thankful we are for our modern means of transportation when we think of the discomfort endured by those travelers of pioneer days.

TRUE TALES To Live By

Chief White Pigeon, Heroic Indian Chief

While traveling through southwest Michigan some years ago, I drove into the town of White Pigeon. On inquiring about the significance of the name of the town, I was told an amazing story.

This part of Michigan was once inhabited by Indians of the Potowatome Tribe and also by a group of white settlers. There was no antagonism between them, largely because the chief of the Potowatome had a friendly relationship with his white neighbors. The children of the settlers, too, loved Chief White Pigeon, and often played among the tepees with the Indian children.

One day, as the head of his tribe, Chief White Pigeon attended a council meeting of the chiefs of all the tribes in the area. The meeting was held some hundred miles to the northeast of the Potowatome encampment.

At this meeting, Chief White Pigeon was shocked to learn that a raid was being planned by all of the Indian tribes of the area against the white settlers. He was convinced that the attack would result in a massacre of the men, women and children who had long been his friends. The white settlers, as well as the Indians of his tribe, would be taken by surprise and would be unable to defend themselves. He must not let that terrible event take place.

Although he argued strongly against such action, he was outnumbered and the chiefs retired to their tents that night planning to return to their tribes the next morning to organize the attack.

Aware of White Pigeon's opposition to the massacre, the horses were kept under guard. However, the Indian chief was able to sneak out of camp under cover of darkness and to make his way on foot to warn his white friends of the danger that threatened them. Fortunately, he soon had enough moonlight to help him find his way through the forests and around the swamps on that hazardous journey.

Swimming the streams and following forest paths through the woods that were sometimes blocked by fallen trees and tangled bushes that tore at his body, the fleet-footed White Pigeon ran, hour after hour, seldom stopping to rest.

At times he became so exhausted that he was forced to stop for a few moments to regain his strength. But there continually ran through his mind thoughts of his white friends, especially the children, who would be tortured and killed if he didn't reach the settlement in time to warn them.

Finally, after a grueling run of over a hundred miles, the gallant White Pigeon staggered into the white settlement. Just as he uttered the warning of the threatened Indian attack, Chief White Pigeon's heart gave out and he fell dead. He had given his life to save his friends.

I was so moved by this touching story of Chief White Pigeon that I drove to a small park on the outskirts of the town. There stood a stone with the following engraving:

"In Memory of Wahbameme, Chief White Pigeon
Who Gave His Life to Save the Settlers of This Place
Greater Love Hath No Man Than This
That a Man Lay Down His Life for His friends."

Chief Black Hawk, Fighter for Indian Rights

In the park overlooking Black Hawk Lake in Lake View, Iowa, is the statue of a famous Indian chief, Black Hawk. I was curious about the reason for the statue so I did a bit of research about his life.

He was the chief of the Sauk Tribe , which once pitched their wigwams in the Lake View area. This famous Indian warrior spent most of his life battling with the white man in defense of what was considered to be Indian territory. Yet he fought also with several Indian tribes. He battled the Osage, the Cherokee, the Menominee and the Dakotas, and was proud of his accomplishments in winning almost all of

TRUE TALES To Live By

his battles. One would think that all of the Indian tribes would unite in the effort to defeat their common enemy. Yet they fought with and killed each other.

Battles between Indian tribes were often over which methods should be used to fight the white invaders and to punish those who trespassed on their hunting grounds. Black Hawk stated that all his wars with Indians were caused by the relatives of those who were killed or by aggression on their hunting grounds.

When the Sauk Tribe returned from a hunting expedition, they brought dried buffalo meat and deer meat and Sioux scalps of those who had been found trespassing on their hunting grounds. Each party knew that the other had a right to retaliate and avenge the death of their relatives after each battle.

Chief Black Hawk's battles were with both Indian tribes and American soldiers. Although he was proud to proclaim that he could usually defeat Indian tribes, he acknowledged that when it came to fighting his greatest enemies, the Americans, the outcome was different. He said, "There are more Americans than leaves on the trees."

Chief Black Hawk had the reputation of being a skilled warrior. He was once pursued by an army whose members included Abraham Lincoln and Lieutenant Jefferson Davis. He also fought troops under Zachary Taylor, who became an American president. He defeated Zachary Taylor in that battle.

He carried on a lifetime dispute with Chief Keokuk, another Sauk warrior, about the best way to face the threat of extinction, and saw his tribe split forever because of this rivalry.

Chief Black Hawk, like most of the Indians, worshipped the Great Spirit who they believed created the world. Here is a quote from Chief Black Hawk's biography:

"Some Indians believe in two Spirits; one good and one bad, and make feasts for the Bad Spirit to keep him quiet! Then they can make peace with the Good Spirit who will not hurt them."

Isn't this similar to the devil worshippers of our day who consider murder a part of their rites?

Chief Black Hawk knew Chicago when it was a cluster of log huts around a fort. It is difficult to imagine the city of Chicago with its crowded traffic and towering skyscrapers as once being only a cluster of log houses on the shores of Lake Michigan.

In my school days, the general impression I had of the Indians was that many of them were savages who massacred women and children and were proud of the scalps they were able to collect from their victims.

It may come as a shock to learn that there were American soldiers who were involved in massacring the Indians. One such horrible event was when President Jackson, to punish Black Hawk's people, ordered his soldiers to overtake a fleeing band of Sauk families, struggling to escape by crossing the Mississippi River. The Indians raised a white flag of truce that the American soldiers did not honor. Men, women and children were slaughtered.

There is the shameful account of how the women of the Sauk Tribe tried to swim across the broad Mississippi on the northeastern border of Iowa with their babies on their backs. Many of them drowned with their babies in an attempt to escape the American soldiers. The Americans won that battle but it was a victory of which they had no reason to be proud.

Eventually Black Hawk was captured and spent several years in jail. On his release, he was taken on a fantastic tour of several eastern cities. Crowds gathered in Philadelphia, Baltimore and New York to cheer the famous Indian chief.

In view of the atrocities he had committed, it seems strange that people would cheer the man who had led men, women and children of his tribe to slaughter.

TRUE TALES To Live By
Friendly Wolf

This section of the book is entitled "True Tales of Pioneer Days," and I have endeavored to report stories, which are true, not fiction. The story I am about to relate is a folk tale, but the telling of it is true in that it is one of the stories that Blackfoot Indian mothers often told to their children.

During my boyhood, when I read about the American Indian, I had a picture of families living in wigwams or tepees. The weapons the Indian men used for hunting and for warfare were the spear and the bow and arrow.

The men of the tribe had no knowledge of saddles. They rode their horses bareback. They wore moccasins, and some of the Indians scalped their victims and displayed the scalps before their wigwams as evidence of their bravery. We were told that not all of the Indians resorted to this barbaric practice.

There is a phase of Indian life with which I have not been familiar. The mothers loved their children as the white people did, but I did not realize that they often told the children stories at bedtime, many of them regarded as folk tales.

The most fascinating tale that I have heard was about a friendly wolf. It was often told by Blackfoot Indian mothers to their children.

The story begins when the Blackfoot were moving camp and were attacked by a band of Crow Indians. The Blackfoot were moving in a long line with the old men and women and children in the middle. The warriors were in the front and rear.

The Crows attacked the women and children and killed many and took others captive before the Blackfoot warriors were able to drive them off.

According to the tale that the Blackfoot told, one of the captives was a woman whose name was Sits-By-The-Door. She was given into the custody of a Crow warrior who treated her cruelly. Every night her feet were tied together and a rope around her waist was fastened to the wife of the warrior to keep her from escaping.

The Crow woman was very sympathetic to the woman in her charge. One night she overheard her husband plotting to kill his prisoner. No reason is given for his evil intention.

That night when the deep breathing of her husband convinced her that he was sound asleep, she loosened the ropes and set the woman free. She gave her a pair of moccasins, a flint and a sack of food to help her on the journey back to her tribe.

The frightened woman traveled all night, hoping that pursuers would not be able to catch up with her. During four nights she traveled, hiding in the underbrush during the day. Her supply of food was exhausted and she became so weak that she was hardly able to walk. There were holes in her moccasins and her feet were cut and bleeding.

As she lay down exhausted, to take a brief rest, she was alarmed to see a huge wolf approaching her from the bushes. In her weakened condition she tried to run from the beast but collapsed on the ground. As the wolf drew near, she again attempted to run from him. As she stumbled along between the trees, the wolf kept following her, always keeping a short distance away.

Finally, the poor woman gave up in despair and sank to the ground. Now she knew that the wolf was about to attack her. However, to her surprise, he crept closer to her and lay down at her feet.

Finally, she spoke to him and in a weak pleading voice begged him to get her some food although she had no hope that he would respond. In a few minutes, he trotted away and soon returned with a buffalo calf he had killed. He laid the calf at her feet.

With the help of the flint her friend had given her, she was able to start a fire and cook a meal. She offered a part of it to the friendly wolf. Refreshed, she continued on her way with the wolf following close behind.

TRUE TALES To Live By

At last she found her way to the Blackfoot camp, told her friends how the wolf had saved her life and begged them to treat him kindly. He was accepted into the camp by the children who loved the friendly wolf.

One day, Sits-By-The-Door fell sick and was confined to her teepee. The dogs did not like the wolf intruder and drove him from the camp. Every evening, the friendly wolf would come to the top of a hill near the encampment and look longingly at the teepee where his friend lay ill.

Although the children brought him food each day, he finally disappeared and was seen no more. We can picture the children sitting wide-eyed about the campfire as their mothers tell them this touching story about the friendly wolf.

Massacre Threat at Fort Madison

Those who are interested in the early history of Iowa will probably be familiar with the following tale of Fort Madison that is now known as the city where the Iowa State Penitentiary is located.

It was in 1808 that the U.S. Government decided to build a trading post and a fort known as Fort Madison. The Sac and the Fox Indians resented this enterprise for they disliked having soldiers and forts on their land.

Lieutenant Alpha Kingsley explained to them that the trading post was for the purpose of doing business with the Indians and that the soldiers at the fort were no threat to them, but the Indians refused to believe him. They protested so strongly that the trading post was finally built about one hundred yards from the fort, which was surrounded by a stockade fourteen feet high.

The Indians decided that their only hope of driving away the soldiers was to destroy the fort. They knew that would be a very difficult undertaking so they devised a scheme by which they could gain entrance to the fort, kill the soldiers stationed there, and burn the fort.

The warriors decided this could easily be accomplished by a friendly gesture. They would offer to give an Indian dance inside the stockade for the entertainment of the soldiers stationed there. The soldiers looked forward to the coming of the Indians, for there was little entertainment for them in this isolated location. The plan of the *friendly* visitors was that weapons would be hidden beneath their blankets; then in the midst of their dance, at a given signal, the soldiers would be attacked and the fort burned. The braves were convinced that this trick would result in the death of all the soldiers in the fort.

Black Hawk, the chief of the Indians, gathered with his warriors at the appointed time before the gate of the stockade, waiting for permission to enter. When the gate was opened, instead of being greeted by the friendly soldiers, they found to their dismay that they faced a loaded cannon. They had no choice but to retreat.

The Indians were unaware that one of their tribe had warned the soldiers of Black Hawk's scheme. A friendly Indian was responsible for saving the lives of all the soldiers at the fort.

In the historical account, there is no reference as to the reason that one of the tribe revealed the secret plan of the attack. It is interesting to speculate about this seemingly unknown factor in that dramatic incident. Had the soldiers befriended one of the warriors and he wished to reciprocate by warning them of the danger that threatened them? Might the *friendly* Indian have been a woman who realized how much grief the wives and children of the soldiers would have suffered if their loved ones had been massacred?

Another unanswered question is whether or not the Indian who revealed the plot was discovered. If so, that one, who to us was a hero, would no doubt have been burned at the stake.

This story of a noble warrior who risked his life to save those who were considered to be his enemies is a thrilling tale that needs to be told to our children and our grandchildren.

TRUE TALES To Live By

The Battle of Bloody Creek

It is well known that the Pilgrims fled from England because they were not allowed to worship as they pleased. I didn't realize until I read excerpts from a friend's genealogy how severe the punishment was for opposition to the Church of England. The following is a quote from a historical report on the persecutions of Christians during the 1600s:

> Any persons who separated themselves from the Church were in danger of accusations of heresy and eventually high treason. This was a dangerous crime. The punishment was death, usually by being burned at the stake.

Do we wonder why the Pilgrims fled on the Mayflower from England if people accused of opposition to the king were burned at the stake?

One of the leaders of the movement against the Church of England was a man by the name of John Lathrop to whom my neighbor is also distantly related. The father of nine children, Lathrop was imprisoned for months in Clink Prison. That is probably how we got the expression, "He was thrown in the clink."

Clink Prison has a history similar to that of the Tower of London, where many famous persons were beheaded. I had the privilege years ago of visiting the famous Tower of London. It was during the reign of King Henry VIII that two queens, Anne Boelyn and Catherine Howard, were beheaded in this famous prison for misconduct. It is understandable, perhaps, why murderers were beheaded, but for a queen to be beheaded is preposterous!

During John Lathrop's imprisonment, he learned that his wife, Hannah, was very ill and near death. He was released from prison until she died and then returned to jail. His children sent a petition to the king through the archbishop, begging for his release. He was finally set free with the understanding that he would not continue to speak against the king's religious beliefs. After his release, however, Lathrop continued encouraging groups whose beliefs were contrary to that of the official Church of England. Strange as it may seem, government police had difficulty in locating his whereabouts, even when using dogs to search. It is interesting to know that dogs were used to hunt lawbreakers over three hundred years ago, as they are today.

Lathrop was finally located, but promised his freedom if he left England and gave up his citizenship. With two hundred fellow passengers, he left for New England in a ship named *The Griffin*. It landed in Boston some fourteen years after the Mayflower reached America.

What courage those forefathers of ours had—to face the dangers and discomforts of an ocean crossing, and to land in a hostile country so that they could practice the Christian faith which meant so much to them!

They suffered not only from starvation and disease but from savage Indian attacks. Our history books tell of some of the Indians who befriended them, such as Chief Massasoit of the Wampanoag tribe of Indians. The chief promised he would not permit his people to harm the Pilgrims as long as he lived. He kept this promise for fifty years. The Pilgrims, in turn, agreed to do all in their power to protect the Indians.

On the first Thanksgiving in 1621, Chief Massasoit spoke these words: "The Great Spirit must love his white children best." There were others among the Indian tribes who made the lives of the Pilgrims very difficult. In fact, there were both good and bad Indians.

When John Lathrop landed in Boston, he had no idea of the heartaches he would suffer because of his loyalty to his faith.

I don't recall reading in my history books about the Battle of Muddy Creek. I learned it in my friend's genealogy. Many of the Pilgrims were living in small settlements. If one village was reported to be in danger of attacks by the Indians, each of the villages would send men to help in the defense of the Pilgrim families.

One of these battles was fought on the shores of a stream known as Muddy Creek. Thomas Lathrop, the son of John Lathrop, led a group of sixty men to help defend one of the villages from an attack by the Indians. The savages learned of the plans and attacked the men as they were crossing the creek. The Indians slaughtered all sixty, including their leader, Thomas Lathrop. Since that time, the river has been called Bloody Creek.

The devotion of our Puritan fathers to their Christian belief, and the dreadful price they paid for that devotion, should make us appreciate all the more the freedom we have today to practice our faith.

Southern Swamps: Beautiful but Dangerous

There was a time when ponds covered much of Iowa. Farmers traveling by horse and wagon from Manson to Rockwell City had to drive around several ponds to reach their destination. Even in my youth, back in the early 1900's, I remember a neighbor telling how he could ice skate on a string of connected ponds from his farm home to Pomeroy—a distance of four miles. All those ponds have been drained now and yield abundant crops of corn and soybeans.

Down in the southern states, however, many swamps still remain, covering thousands of acres. On a recent trip to Mississippi, we drove over a swamp where the highway was built on pillars. It was a four-lane highway where the median was not covered with grass, as in the Midwest. Instead, it was swampland. We didn't check the mileage, but I would estimate the distance over that swamp to be about twenty miles.

During our brief stay in the South, I was fascinated by the stories I heard and read of the many swamps in the Southland. Even though the water may be a deep black color, to the casual observer, a swamp may seem like a picture book scene with beautiful Spanish moss ornamenting the cypress trees. But the swamp can be a forbidden land that can swallow those who carelessly invade it.

Many of the swamps are populated with stinkpot turtles, hundreds of alligators and copperhead snakes, which are very poisonous. One man reported seeing two hundred alligators in one day. One might think that you could easily outrun a clumsy alligator, but those who live in that area report that an alligator can run very fast for the first twenty-five or thirty-five feet, easily catching an unsuspecting observer. A lady in Alabama who lived near a pond on her farm said she once lost a calf to an alligator.

Until recently, black bears were plentiful in the swamps, and some are seen there today. They find honey in hollow trees. In 1890, a pioneer survey party reported near drowning incidents and encounters with bears, alligators and packs of wild dogs. One man said he nearly drowned when he stepped on what he thought was a mound of dirt and sank in it up to his chin.

On Cowhouse Island in the Okefenokee Swamp, a farmer living near the swamp reported that he lost over a hundred hogs to alligators and bears in three months. One farmer was so angry when he discovered a bear attacking one of his hogs that he fought the animal with a big stick, killing it after a fierce struggle.

Although some of the pioneer farmers lived near the swamps, there were some hardy souls who made a living in the heart of the swamps. In the early 1850s, there lived a family who cleared some of the land on an island in the Okefenokee Swamp and built a home there. The family included fourteen children.

The family must have depended mostly on fish and crocodiles and some garden products for food. Possibly there was a market for the fish among farmers along the shore. That was before the outbreak of the Civil War, when there were no government handouts.

TRUE TALES To Live By

On a visit to the swamps in the southern states, one is impressed by the beauty of the flowers and the birds. A writer of a bird guide has set up listening posts in one of the swamps. He reported seeing fifty-two species of birds. Among them were the yellow-billed cuckoo, the red-bellied woodpecker, the wood thrush, the blue jay, the Carolina chickadee and the yellow-throated warbler.

Among the many kinds of flowers in the swamp are the yellow jasmine, the flowering dogwood, the southern magnolia and the butterfly orchid. The swamps are beautiful.

Many stories have been told of those who ventured into the swamp and never returned. Among the courageous ones who dared to seek refuge in these murky waters have been convicts who escaped from prison. How could they hide in these vast, flooded areas?

They stole boats or made makeshift rafts with which they could reach one of the small islands in the area. They obtained food to keep from starving. They depended on fishing or ventured on shore to steal supplies from farmers who lived near the swamps. Some of these convicts were captured and returned to prison; few ever made it to freedom.

There were those who existed by making liquor. In the days when it was unlawful to sell intoxicating homemade brew, the bootleggers made arrangements to accommodate their customers in secret hiding places. An empty jug was placed in a stump or a hollow tree. Several hours later, it would be filled, to quench the thirst of the men on shore who had left the cash to pay for it.

There were also deserters from the Confederate Army who were not in sympathy with the rebel cause. They tried to escape the bloody battles of that terrible war by hiding out in the swamps.

Before and during the Civil War, the swamps were an important refuge for runaway slaves seeking their freedom. We can understand how the slaves could follow an underground railway to homes where the people were eager to receive and protect them in their flight to the North. But how could they hide in a gloomy swamp where there were no friends to assist them? In a book entitled, *The Great Cypress Swamps*, by John Dennis, reference is made to how escaping slaves followed a river to the north. They sometimes hid in the swamps where it was difficult for their pursuers and dogs to find them. Often the fugitives were captured and returned to their masters who treated them cruelly for trying to escape.

There were many friends of the slaves, who at the risk of their lives, assisted in their desperate flight to freedom. There were others who made their living capturing the runaway slaves. On the Delaware Maryland Railroad Line, there lived a notorious character by the name of Patty Cannon. She operated an inn and had no qualms about murdering some of her guests if she could be paid for it. She was known as a murderer for hire.

This evil woman had a gang of desperados in her employ whose main assignment was to capture slaves. In 1829, she was finally arrested and sentenced to be hanged. Three weeks before her execution, to escape the hangman's noose, she managed to take a fatal dose of poison.

This hated woman was well known throughout the South. Even the children were aware of her evil doings. Often when little children were misbehaving, their black mother would quiet them with the words: "Hush, or Patty Cannon will get you."

The runaway slaves and escaped criminals who took refuge in the swamps probably didn't see the beauty of their surroundings. To them it was ugly and dangerous. It was a temporary refuge but also a place of snakes and alligators where a person could disappear in the murky waters.

To others, the swamps have a rare beauty with beautiful cypress trees decorated with Spanish moss and lovely flowers and birds to delight the eye. I can understand why there are those who feel the swamps of the Southland should be preserved for posterity.

TRUE TALES To Live By

The Buffalo Hunt

About a mile east of our home is a quarter section of land that is virgin prairie. A plow has never been used to break the sod. No crops have ever been harvested from it except some hay.

A farmer by the name of Otto Kalsow, who owned the prairie when I was a boy, could have made a good income from that land. It would no doubt have raised bumper crops of corn.

There was a time many years ago before pioneer settlers came to this area when Indians occupied the land. It is a possibility that Indians pitched their wigwams here. I like to visualize the warriors beating their drums and staging their dances on the land that is now known as the Kalsow Prairie.

In those early days, herds of buffalo roamed the prairie. My dad broke the sod on the farm where I lived as a boy. He didn't see buffalo, but in the cold winter months he wore a long coat made of buffalo hide.

The Indians depended on the wild buffalo for their living. Besides the meat of the buffalo, almost every part of the animal had a purpose. The droppings, when dry, provided fuel for cooking. Hoes were made of the shoulder blades. Sinews were a part of the bow. Horns were made into cups for holding food. From the ribs were carved out arrowheads. Even the tail had a use. It made a good fly swatter.

I had always thought that the main way of killing the buffalo was with the bow and arrow. But another very effective method was used in mountain country. The buffalo were stampeded and driven over a cliff. Picture a herd of a hundred or more buffalo being chased over a cliff and hurtling, head over heels, over a sheer drop of a hundred feet or more. The hunters were waiting below to butcher the killed or wounded animals.

In another method of hunting, two Indians would approach a buffalo herd, each crawling on all fours under a wolf skin and head. When they were close enough to their victim, they could kill him with a bow and arrow.

That method of hunting was evidently used before the appearance of the horse. It would be quite easy to ride a horse along the side of a running animal and dispatch him quickly with a bow and arrow or a spear. Without a horse, other methods had to be used.

Pioneers Had Reason To Be Thankful

We have been writing about the difference between our life today and that of the pioneers of a century ago. We need to be aware, however, that there are areas in the world where modern life is as primitive as, or worse than it was in America during the days of the pioneers.

A television commentator recently made the statement that half of the people of the world eat with their fingers. I have visited parts of Africa where the daily existence is more difficult than my grandfather's was. Would we rather live in a sod house than in a grass hut? Would we prefer to live in a log cabin, or sleep out in the open and then die from lack of food, like thousands have done in southern Africa in recent months.

A recent newspaper item reports that in some countries in northwest Africa, soldiers not only kill their prisoners, but they eat them! Evidently cannibalism is not only a custom of the past.

We don't want to give a wrong picture of China or Africa, for many of its cities are as modern as ours. But there is another side to life in China of which we privileged Americans should be aware.

Doris Ekblad, a missionary from the Evangelical Free Church in Knowloon, Hong Kong, described to us her experience traveling *economy style* in China. Train tickets are not

TRUE TALES To Live By

available until seven o'clock in the morning on the day of travel, with ticket lines beginning to form at midnight the night before! Finally, at seven, the ticket window opens and someone announces, "All sold out!"

According to Doris, it was a challenge to get on a train without breaking or spraining a limb, or losing your luggage or glasses in the crush. There was a desperate scramble to get a seat. Many climbed in through the train windows, some carrying huge sacks of eggplant, potatoes and cabbage, plus baggage.

All train stations swarmed with masses of humanity. When the train arrived in Beijing at five o'clock one morning, the broad paved expanse in front of the train station was so covered with sleeping bodies they had to carefully step around them. People were sleeping on just scraps of newspaper on the bare ground. Appalled Doris asked, "Where do they all go when it rains?" Her friend shook her head. "They all come looking for work. Many die here."

That morning, an old man came, offering a live baby he had found in the garbage. "Will someone take this baby?" There were no takers. Another such baby was brought to the police within the hour, also found back in the garbage.

Missionaries found the poverty level in China calculated so differently from back where they lived. There are places where the whole family has just one pair of pants to share. Whoever must go out to the street takes his turn wearing them! Never mind size, pant legs were rolled up or down to fit!

This description of traveling by train, economy class, reminded me of the time I traveled from Algeria to Morocco, economy class, some years ago. As I remember the cost was about a cent a mile. There were no seats. Turbaned passengers sat on the floor. A man next to me held eight or ten live chickens, their feet tied together with a string, as his baggage. I traveled that way, not only to save expenses, but

SKIP WESTPHAL

also to see what many Arabs experience when they travel in their country.

Although this picture of modern life in some lands beyond the seas is a gruesome one, it is interesting for all of us to be aware of how much improved the life our pioneer ancestors was to that of many people in the world today.

Pilgrim Encounters Stormy Sea in 1620

In previous stories of the early pioneer days, I have written for the most part about life at the time of the Civil War and into the beginning of the 1900s. In this episode, we will go back three hundred and seventy-five years to the landing of the pilgrims in 1620.

A friend of mine has done a great deal of research into that period of American history and has discovered several interesting incidents that are not found in our history books.

Nearly everyone is familiar with the experience of these early settlers who sailed the seas to escape the persecution at the hands of the British king. Anyone who tried to establish a religion other than that of the official Church of England was considered a traitor. Many of these so-called *rebels* were imprisoned for their religious activities.

It took a great deal of courage for those 102 Pilgrims to set out across the ocean in a small ship for an unknown land.

One of the frightening experiences described in my friend's genealogy was the Mayflower's encounter of a violent storm in mid-Atlantic. A young man named John Howland was almost drowned when a mountainous wave swept him overboard. Following is the description of his narrow escape:

"Grasping a rope which was trailing astern of the ship, although at first he was several fathoms under water, he finally managed to haul himself to the surface. He was then rescued by means of a boat hook along with a rope."

In William Bradford's journal, this frightening incident is described as follows: "It pleased God, that tho' somewhat ill upon it, he lived many years, and became a useful member both in church and Commonwealth. He was Deputy and Assistant the greater part of his long and useful life and was one of the leading men in the Colony, also a partaker of their hazardous undertakings and eminent for his devotion to its interests.

Also aboard the ship was a fourteen-year old girl, Elizabeth Tilley, whom Bradford married after they landed on the shores of New England. Elizabeth lost both her father and her mother during the first year of the Pilgrim's landing.

Of the 102 who crossed the ocean on the Mayflower, fifty died during that first winter. It was said they succumbed to a fatal sickness, but the deaths were due largely to starvation and the bitter cold winter. The lack of food was such a problem that there were times when each one, including the children, were allotted only five kernels of corn for one meal. It is hardly surprising that many of them died from starvation.

Why should I be interested in the frightening experiences of the young man, John Howland, who was almost drowned when a wave swept him overboard during a frightening storm? Why should I be interested in the fourteen-year-old girl, Elizabeth Tilley, who lost her parents during that first terrible winter and later married John Howland?

It so happens that I have a neighbor, an Iowa farmer, who is a descendent of John Howland and Elizabeth Tilley. It's amazing how these genealogies can unearth such interesting stories and bring them back to us after several hundred years.

SKIP WESTPHAL

Thirty-Nine Indians Hanged on a Single Scaffold

While the Civil War was raging in the South, a battle was being fought here in the Midwest—specifically in Minnesota, but it wasn't a battle between the Union soldiers and the Confederate rebels. It was a struggle between the white settlers and the Sioux Indians under the leadership of Chief Little Crow.

Drive through the towns and cities of southern Minnesota, with their stores, restaurants, filling stations and teeming traffic, and it becomes difficult to imagine there was a day when the area's residents were terrified by reports of Indian attacks.

Take, for example, the attack on New Ulm, Minnesota, during the summer of 1862. Chief Little Crow had come to parley with a trader about obtaining food for his people. The trader, Andrew Myrick, was reported to have said, "As far as I am concerned, if the Indians are hungry, let them eat grass."

As it states in the Bible in James 3:6, "The tongue is a fire." And indeed, Myricks's words started a fire. The Sioux were moved to attack the settlers in New York. A courageous Paul Revere from New York rode under cover of darkness and warned the people of the coming attack. Armed settlers of nearby towns gathered in buggies and on horseback and started out for New Ulm. When they arrived, they found that many houses had already been set on fire.

Before long, the Indians had completely encircled the town. When they got within rifle shot, they let out a war whoop and attacked the town from every direction. The beleaguered settlers tore doors off houses to use for stretchers to carry the wounded to hospitals.

The frightened women and children huddled in basements. At the end of the day, the Indians were driven off, but three-fourths of the town lay in ruins.

81

TRUE TALES To Live By

The raiding of farms and settlements continued throughout the whole area, as far south as the Iowa border. Thirty thousand people fled their homes. More than a year later, no settlers had returned to nineteen of the twenty-three farms and settlements that had been devastated by Indian attacks. But with great loss of life to men, women, and children, the Indians were finally beaten and many of them captured.

By October, two thousand of the Indians had been tried in court and 306 were sentenced to hang, but President Lincoln decreed they should be treated as prisoners of war. They were brought to trial again and forty were sentenced to be hanged. One of them was later pardoned.

On December 16, 1862, the remaining thirty-nine Indians were hanged on a single scaffold in Mankato.

Boom Towns of the West

Thousands of prospectors poured into Arizona seeking their fortunes in gold. The would-be millionaires heard about towns where you could wash your face at the end of the day and pan four ounces of gold from your whiskers. These gold hunters came from all points of the globe expecting to get rich quick.

In these boomtowns, the first place of business was a saloon that often consisted of two whiskey barrels with a plank stretched between them. This set-up served as a bar.

The mining camps were populated by a ramshackle collection of boisterous, dirty, devil-may-care reprobates. Some struck it rich, but most of those who did were the ones who came in, not to pull the rich ore from the earth, but to remove it from the pockets of the lucky miners. It was called *mining the miners.*

Many of the prospectors made a fortune in gold but lost most of it to the gamblers and the operators of the saloons. The ladies who populated the bars took what was left and sent the prospectors scurrying off to the hills for more yellow dust. No wonder they were referred to as *jackass prospectors.*

Someone remarked to me the other day, "We don't have saloons today; they are called bars; but we have many restaurants, gas stations and grocery stores that take the place of the saloons of those early days."

A Tucson newspaper in those gold rush days published a letter from a resident of Tombstone, Arizona, reporting that the town had a population of fifteen hundred people, with a dozen gambling houses, more than twenty saloons, and over five hundred gamblers. The writer of the letter commented that there was still hope, for he knew of two Bibles in the town.

Imagine twenty saloons in a town of fifteen hundred!

Honeymoon Almost Ends in Disaster

Among the dangers the early settlers feared in the Iowa of a century or more ago was the howling blizzards that swept through the prairie. The storms were more severe in those days, due in part to a lack of trees that served as windbreaks.

There are many stories told about frightening experiences during these winter storms. A story appeared in the Manson, Iowa, Journal in a series entitled, "The Winning of the West" published in 1924.

It was in December of 1864 that a young couple, Mr. and Mrs. Levi Davis, was on their way home from a honeymoon trip.

They were traveling in an open buggy, pulled by a team of horses. It began to snow and the temperature had dropped to thirty degrees below zero. Fortunately, they reached the stage coach station at Twin Lakes, and the driver decided that they should stay for the night.

TRUE TALES To Live By

The next morning, they decided to continue their journey although the temperature was still twenty-eight degrees below zero. Just as they reached a hill near what was known as Hell Slough, the rear axle broke.

The driver left the buggy robes to keep the couple warm and headed with the horses to the nearest town, Sac City, Iowa, to look for help. Fortunately, there was an old abandoned dry well near the road. The couple crawled down into the well, with the aid of a rope, grateful for the shelter from the wind and bitter cold.

The bride's feet were nearly frozen and they both feared they would be so bitterly frost bitten that her feet would have to be amputated. What a way to spend a honeymoon in the bottom of a well!

By desperately rubbing her feet, they finally succeeded in bringing back the circulation. Hoping that someone would come to their rescue, they climbed out of the well. The husband used the buffalo robes to make a shelter, hoping that any travelers passing by would rescue them. Their shelter was partly hidden by tall grass. The husband walked to the top of the hill where he had left some of the buffalo robes.

Suddenly, Mrs. Davis heard the sound of horse hoofs on the road. She peered through the tall grass to see who was approaching. It was the presiding elder of the Methodist churches in the area. On seeing something peering through the tall grass, the pastor assumed it was some wild animal.

He reached for his rifle, took aim and was about to pull the trigger when he realized that the creature was not a wild animal but a woman. The honeymoon almost ended tragically.

Although the pastor offered the couple a ride, a wagon appeared with soldiers headed for Sac City. They took the couple to the nearest town. There is no record of how the bride and groom reached their home, but they no doubt were very grateful for the miraculous way in which they concluded their journey.

SKIP WESTPHAL

Murder Not a Crime?

The disturbing problems that beset us today may lead us to conclude that our world is growing steadily worse. It is a good practice for us to do some exploring now and then into the early history of our country. Such a study will help us to see and appreciate the progress we have made in learning how to get along with each other.

On a visit to New Orleans, I had the opportunity to visit a park known as The Oaks. It was once a heavily wooded section of land on the outskirts of the city where antagonists met to settle their arguments by dueling. Here, for months on end, not a day passed without a duel being fought.

It was a common sight for those who lived near The Oaks to see carriages drive early in the morning outside the city and then to see them return a half hour later taking home the dead and the wounded.

During the 1830s more duels were fought in New Orleans than in any other city in the world. On one Sunday in 1939, ten duels were fought in one day, one of them between a father and his son. The common acceptance of this practice is shown by the fact that Governor Claiborne of Louisiana once fought in a duel, and his brother-in-law was killed in one. Imagine the governor of our state taking part in a duel to the death with a political opponent.

Many of the reasons for these bloody fights seem laughable, in spite of their disastrous results. A Neapolitan nobleman fought in fourteen duels because of arguments over who was the greater poet, Dante or Ariosto. A young man evidently used his sense of humor to get the better of his good judgment when he sent a letter to a lady reading:

"Your face is round and red and fat.
Like pulpit cushions, or redder than that."

It was a quotation from an old song entitled, *Sweet Kitty Clover*. The lady's brother challenged the joker to a duel over this affair but no one was injured as the seconds purposely neglected to load the pistols. This so angered the challenger that he insisted on a fight with one of the seconds, his best friend, who was killed as a result.

In the days of the Old West, the attitude toward murder was similar in some respects to the practice of dueling in the Deep South. When two outlaws—or even respectable citizens—faced each other with six shooters in their belts, determined to shoot it out, and one of them was killed, the one who survived was not arrested for murder. That method of settling quarrels was generally accepted. In some respects, our modern way of living is an improvement over that of the days of the Wild West and the time in the deep South prior to the Civil War.

Indians a Threat to Pioneer Preachers

One of the most interesting chapters in American history involves the dangers and the hardships faced by the circuit riders in those early pioneer days. There were times when American Indians were sometimes a threat to hearty souls who carried the gospel by horseback from one settlement to another. They were brave men, those circuit riders.

There is the experience of a preacher by the name of Pleasant Tackett who, while on his way by mule-back to preach in one of the pioneer homes in his area, was chased by a band of American Indians. They were closing in on Pastor Tackett and the arrows were flying overhead. The preacher was urging his steed to increase his speed but evidently his mule didn't sense the danger he and his rider were in.

Suddenly the preacher felt a sharp pain in his leg and he realized that one of the arrows had hit its mark. With a desperate effort, he pulled the arrow from his leg and used it as a whip to urge his mule to a faster gallop.

That arrow probably saved the preacher's life for he outdistanced his pursuers and made his escape. For a mule to be able to outdistance the fleet-footed American Indian ponies is nothing short of a miracle. We are not told the rest of the story, but possibly the preacher was approaching a settlement and the pursuing band decided to give up.

I would think that Pastor Tackett would have kept that arrow as a souvenir. I know if that frightening experience had happened to me, I would have kept that arrow to show my friends and tell them how it had saved me. It must have been exciting to be a preacher in those days.

The life of a circuit rider, however, was not always exciting.

One famous traveling preacher, Peter Cartright, wrote of his travels. "We crossed creeks and large rivers without bridges or ferry boats. Often we swam them on horseback or crossed on trees that had fallen over the streams. Sometimes we drove our horses over, and often waded out waist deep. If by chance we got a dugout, or canoe, to cross in ourselves and swim our horses by, it was quite a treat."

Methodist Horace Bishop told of making the rounds of his circuit. "I never took breakfast and dinner at the same place except on Friday, which was laundry day in the country …My wardrobe was one end of my saddle-bag, my bookcase the other end…My study was the shade of any tree on the way to my appointments, where there was grass for my horse…I slept wherever it was convenient, on a sheepskin or on my Mexican blanket, occasionally on a dirt or a puncheon floor."

One circuit rider estimated that the bare earth was their bed three fourths of the time, winter or summer, with "a saddle for their pillow and the sky for their coverlet."

Travelers rarely found comfortable accommodations. Housing space on the frontier was always at a premium, limited as a rule, to bare family necessities. Bishop Asbury wrote of the generous, but poor pioneers: "But kindness will not make a crowded log cabin, 12 feet by 10 agreeable. Without are cold and rain, and within, six adults and as many children, one of which is all motion. The dogs too sometimes must be admitted. I found that among my other trials, I had taken the itch." Considering the many dirty beds the bishop had slept in, he marveled that he had not caught it twenty times more.

A story is told of a pastor who, while lecturing on the evils of strong drink displayed in two glass jars. One was filled with water, the other with whiskey. A worm was placed in the water jar and it obviously was not affected by it. Then it was dropped into the jar filled with whiskey and it inevitably shriveled up.

"What lesson do we learn from this demonstration?" the preacher asked.

A man in the back row rose to his feet and drawled, "We learn that if you drink enough whiskey, it will kill all your worms."

To those pioneer circuit riders who preached 'the gospel' so fearlessly, drunkenness was no joke, intoxicating liquor was one of the worst evils of the day. It was referred to as *the demon rum.* Bar room fights were common and they often resulted in murder.

A drunk, however, was not the threat that he is today. If he was able to mount his horse, he could reach home without any danger to others. The modern drunk behind the wheel of a car is a threat to the safety of other travelers on the highway.

How surprised those pioneer ministers of 'the gospel' would have been had they known that a time would come in our country when thousands upon thousands of men, women and little children would be crippled for life or killed every year by the *demon rum,* sold not only in saloons as it was then, but in grocery stores across the land.

The pay the circuit riders received was far from adequate. The yearly salary of Methodist circuit riders prior to 1800 was sixty-four dollars. During the 1800s it was raised to eighty dollars. One of those pioneer preachers observed that during a year of preaching, he received a total of "eight dollars and twelve watermelons."

Those pioneer worship services were often interrupted. One preacher reported that he was about halfway through his sermon when the dogs who had followed their masters to church had come upon a bear in a nearby woods. The minister stopped his sermon and announced that the church service would be resumed later. The men of the congregation joined him with their guns to get that bear. The women stayed behind to pray.

After they got the bear, the preacher returned to his pulpit and completed his sermon. Evidently they used the bear for food.

There were times when the congregations of the circuit riders failed to get the preacher's message. A pastor was preaching one day about the importance of forgiveness and asked all present who had overcome this unchristian feeling of dislike to stand.

Only one man stood up. He was the oldest man in the community.

"You don't hate anybody?" the preacher asked.

"No, Sir."

"That's a wonderful testimonial," the preacher beamed. "Would you tell why that is?"

"Well, all of them skunks who done me dirt, all them scoundrels I hated," he interrupted himself to cackle triumphantly, "they're all dead."

One of the ways to describe the kind of message the circuit riders preached is to compare it to that of Billy Graham, America's most popular evangelist.

It was customary in those early days for the circuit riders to conduct a *camp meeting*

Often the families brought their picnic baskets and made a day of it. These evangelistic meetings were very effective in combating the lawlessness that was promoted by the saloons of the nineteenth century.

TRUE TALES To Live By

On a Trap Door to China

Several years ago, I had the experience of working for a brief time as a lumberjack. I had done some research on the history of logging and found it to be an interesting chapter in the history of pioneer life on the West Coast in California and Washington.

Dragging the logs out of the forest with several yokes of oxen was a very slow and laborious process. Running water into the top of the trough helped the timber slide smoothly, and it would usually take only a few minutes for the logs to reach the bottom of the hillside, instead of the hours required with teams of slow, plodding oxen.

A narrow catwalk ran beside the flume on which a *flume tender* could walk. His job was to break loose the logs if they jammed when coming around a bend. This was a very dangerous occupation, especially during rainy or icy weather, for the catwalk was only eight to ten inches wide. The posts holding up the flume were often ten or more feet long, and a fall could easily injure or kill a flume tender.

The flumes were sometimes used for other purposes besides transporting logs. There were little boats that carried boxes of groceries or catches of fish, and occasionally an injured logger who was in need of a doctor. The speed on some of these chutes reached sixty miles an hour. The longest chute was the flume at Sanger, California. It was over fifty-four miles long.

During most of the nineteenth century, there were thousands of lumber camps and sawmills along the West Coast, and hundreds of ships were needed to transport the lumber all over the world. There were times when many of the ships were lying idly at anchor, without crews to man them. The reason was that many sailors abandoned ship, thinking the pay would be better and life would be more pleasant in a lumber camp than aboard ship. This problem led to the creation of a new occupation—that of the *crimp*. The job of the crimp was to enlist men to join the crews of the sailing ships. Since many of the men on shore were reluctant to set foot aboard the vessels, the crimp had to use trickery. His method was to offer a prospect a drink, or two or three, and slip chloral hydrate drops into his glass of liquor.

The crimps usually worked in the sleazier saloons that were built along the waterfront. Many of these saloons had back rooms with trap doors arranged conveniently to facilitate the task of getting the unsuspecting drunks aboard ship. These back rooms extended out over the waters of the bay. When the victim was sufficiently tranquilized, he was ready to be shanghaied by the generous friend who had supplied him with drinks. The trap door would suddenly drop open, and the surprised victim would fall into the murky waters below. Men in a boat were ready to fish him out and take him aboard ship where he would be treated to a *cruise* of several weeks or months to some foreign port. In some instances, the shanghaied sailor wouldn't recover from his drunken stupor until he was far out at sea. Soon he would begin to realize that his job for the duration of the voyage would be to swab decks instead of cutting down trees in a lumber camp.

One of the most notorious of these places was the Bucket of Blood Saloon in Everett, Washington. It was built on stilts and extended over the edge of the Snohomish River. Through its trap doors, many a lumberjack who had no hankerin' for the life of a sailor began his career as a shanghaied seaman, helping to transport lumber from the West Coast forests to China, India, South America and other distant ports.

The crimps made a good living in this nefarious business. The police seldom made any efforts to punish the kidnappers, for they knew the economy of the whole West Coast would suffer if too many ships lay idly at anchor. This was one chapter in our country's history where the police were helpless, no matter how much they desired to punish kidnappers.

TRUE TALES To Live By

The Little Professor of Piney Woods

Every state of the union has both good and bad events recorded in its history. Such was true of the story I wrote about the turbulent history of southern Missouri. It is also true of the Deep South that suffered so much during the Civil War and the period following it.

I have been reading recently about some of the hardships Afro-Americans endured even fifty or more years after the slaves had been set free. For many years following the Civil War, they were treated as inferior people.

In the first part of the 1900s, a graduate of the University of Iowa, Lawrence Jones, determined that he could help the people of his own race in the state of Mississippi by organizing a school to give them an educational opportunity. Most of the schools at this time were available only to white people. Lawrence Jones was determined to dedicate his life to this dream.

To make this dream come true, Jones traveled over two Mississippi counties, along the back country trails, from cabin to cabin. He often traveled twenty miles a day, sometimes on mule-back, but usually on foot. He sat with the farmers on their porches in the effort to teach them better farming practices and to interest them in a school for their children. He sometimes mixed pails of white wash and showed them how they could not only improve the looks of their cabins but also keep down the bugs that fed on unfinished logs.

Eventually he was able to start his school of some thirty students, many of them barefooted. They sat on logs around a bonfire at first. Nearby was a deserted sheep shed in which lambs, lizards, snakes and ewes sought shelter. This became the first school building.

A typical incident was that of an old country woman, her feet reddened with blood from her four mile walk that day leading two live geese on a string.

"Fessser," she said, "I'se a widder woman, and this is all I got to give. But I've got nine children and I sho' wants dis school to go up!"

Two geese, a half a hog, 119 pennies and a jug of sorghum were the contributions that came in one day to help the school get going. One of the girl students, Georgia Lee Meyers, had no parents or money. She arrived with a list of friends and the contributions they had made for the Piney Woods School. It was as follows:

> Aunt Hester Robinson—one pound of butter and a dime
>
> Sarah Permill—a chicken
>
> Effie McCoy—a cake and five cents
>
> Bessie Harvey—one of her dresses
>
> Washington Lincoln Johnson—two pecks of meal
>
> Mandy Willis—a dozen eggs

In those days many white folks had a very low opinion of the members of the black race. They were determined to keep them "under the white folks' heel." They didn't approve of the little professor's plan for a school to educate the children of his race. There was talk of getting up a mob to "whip that upstart good" and then send him with a coat of tar and feathers "back to Iowa where he belonged."

But Jones was not deterred by these threats. Once he had to spend a night in a boxcar. Another time he spent the night in jail because a policeman thought all the people of his race should carry passports after dark.

The little professor soon learned that he was not to speak to a white man unless he had been first spoken to. He once commented, "I can understand why a man with a load of manure should go to the back door, but why should a school teacher or a businessman be refused entry to a house by the front door."

The school's enrollment finally grew to 169 students. Barefoot youngsters walked as far as five or six miles a day to school. When the weather was freezing, they wrapped their feet in burlap so as not to miss a day of school.

One day Jones was speaking at a revival meeting in a small country church when he made the remark, "Life is a battleground. We must fight against ignorance and superstition." He didn't realize that some folks would interpret these words to mean that he intended to start a revolution against the white race. It resulted in the most frightening experience of his life for the little professor of Piney Woods.

The Little Professor Is Taken from his Church

As Professor Jones was speaking, two white farm boys, riding past the church on horseback, wondered what the preacher was talking about. They stopped their horses and listened intently at the church door to the voice of the speaker.

They heard him say, "firing line," "wage battle," and "keep fighting." To their ignorant minds, this meant that Jones was planning to start a revolution.

Excitedly, the boys rode from house to house spreading the word that a speaker at the church was urging an armed revolt against the white race.

The next morning, just as the congregation at the church was opening the service by singing their first hymn, their meeting was interrupted by a great deal of commotion and shouting coming from outside. Looking out of the windows, the worshippers were shocked and frightened to see a group of angry looking men surrounding the church.

Suddenly, several men appeared at the door and ordered Jones to come outside. As he stepped out of the door, one of the men threw a rope over his head. With fear clutching at his heart, the little professor realized that he was facing a mob that intended to lynch him. The congregation consisted mostly of elderly folks who were greatly outnumbered by the mob that surrounded the church.

No one spoke as the group slowly walked down the dusty road surrounding their victim. All that could be heard was the hoof beats of the riders who led the way.

Jones was not only frightened by this sudden unbelievable turn of events; he was also puzzled. Why were these angry men doing this? What had he said to arouse such fury in the hearts of these country folk?

As they moved down the road, there came to his mind the words of his father, "What if they lynches a black man every day? How long is Old Glory goin' to be covering a cussed thing like that?"

Then the words of several spirituals he had fervently sung raced through his mind. "Mary don't you weep, don't you mourn," and "Do Lord, oh do Lord, oh do remember me."

Suddenly the group of men stopped at a clearing. In the center was a tree with one limb protruding from it. There was a pile of brush beneath the limb. Were they planning to hang him and then set fire to the brush?

Two teenage boys, shouting gleefully, climbed the tree and threw the end of the rope over the limb. Several men lifted their culprit to the top of the pile of brush and tightened the rope around his neck.

The little professor looked over the crowd of angry faces surrounding him. He knew some of them and wondered how men could be so evil. Then he saw at the edge of the crowd several teenagers who were taking delight in this exciting show. Could these be some of the young people he had worked so hard to give a good education? Was this to be the end of the Piney Woods School that had been his dream for years?

As Professor Jones waited for the rope to tighten around his neck, convinced that he had only seconds to live, he thought of his wife, his white friends, and the eager-eyed children whom he loved. His heart ached for them all.

The Mob shouted, "String him up!"

Just as the rope was being tightened, and Jones knew he had only seconds to live, someone from the crowd jumped up beside the doomed man and waved his hat for attention.

"I want to hear him made a speech befo' we string him up," the man said.

Another agreed, "Yeah, let him talk. Tell us what you told them n_ _ _ _ _ _ at the church."

"Yes," Lawrence cried excitedly. "I'll tell you what I told them."

Never before had he an audience like this —a mob of angry men, faces upturned to receive the impassioned speech of a man with a rope around his neck. He started talking with a fervor he had never felt before. He knew his life probably depended on what he would say in the next few moments.

He talked about his school, of his love for children, about what he was trying to do to make life easier for every one—both black and white. He explained that he had been encouraging a fight—not *against* the white folks but—*for* them, to bring hope and a better life to all the citizens of that great land.

Then he paused for a moment. There was dead silence in that crowd of men who surrounded him. Then in slow measured tones, he made this solemn remark, "There is not a man standing here who wants to go to his God with the blood of an innocent man on his hands."

Again he paused. There was continued dead silence. He could see guilty looks on the faces of the men in that crowd.

Suddenly, an old man wearing a tattered Confederate army coat, elbowed his way through the crowd until he stood beside the man on the top of the brush pile. Carefully he lifted the noose from around his neck and in a soft tone of voice said gently, "Come on down boy. We jes' made a slight mistake."

A shout of approval went up from the crowd as individuals pressed forward to shake the hand of the man they had so recently hated. Some of the younger men seemed disappointed when they realized that they were going to miss the excitement of hanging and burning.

Someone shouted, "Let's help the professor with his school." A hat was passed and the collection totaled over fifty dollars. What a happy turn of events!

Several of the men ushered Lawrence back to the church where several of the congregates had not given up hope but were down on their knees praying for a miracle to save their little professor.

When they saw Jones at the door with several men , they thought at first he was a ghost. Then they ran to him, threw their arms about him and wept for joy. The word spread from cabin to cabin, and parents and children flocked joyously around the *little professor*, to praise the Lord for his escape from death.

What a dramatic story of a man's dedication to the fulfillment of a dream and of God's intervention at a critical moment. There is no doubt but that it was an urging from the Lord which led the old gentleman to loosen the rope around the professor's neck and utter those words, "We jes' made a slight mistake."

AFRICAN ADVENTURES

SKIP WESTPHAL

A Visit to the Land of the Little People

On one of my four visits to Africa, I had the opportunity to meet a Norwegian by the name of Bjorn Figenshou. He had traveled several times to Africa and had mingled on several occasions with the Pygmies of the western Congo.

One day as we were traveling in Figenshou's jeep we drew near to the jungle area inhabited by the Pygmies. I remembered what I had read about the dangers faced by the people in this area. This was the warning.

"If you find it necessary to wade through a swamp or cross a stream as you travel through jungle country, you would do well to beware of crocodiles. They are the largest and perhaps the cruelest of all the reptiles. This loathsome creature will sneak up on you silently under water, grab you by an arm or leg, and pull you under. Often, the only warning of his approach is the ripple of the water above his body as he draws near. The lion, the elephant, and even the snake fear humans, and will keep out of their way if at all possible. But the crocodile is a cruel, treacherous creature which every year devours more people in Africa than all of the lions and leopards put together."

I had also been told that when you hear a faint sound like thunder, you might be hearing the drum beats in a distant Pygmy village.

As we drove along a narrow jungle road, Figenshou realized that we were approaching the area where a Pygmy village was located.

Suddenly he said, "Let's park here beside the road and do a little investigating." We left the jeep and began to follow a path into the jungle. After about a half-hour, we came to an opening in the trees, and there they were. The small group of Pygmies seemed startled at the appearance of strangers, and then one of them evidently recognized Figenshou, for he approached us slowly with a friendly smile.

TRUE TALES To Live By

Pygmies running to meet some friendly visitors who have come to see them.

He spoke a bit of broken English in answer to Figenshou's questions.

Realizing the many dangers which lurk in the dark recesses of this African wilderness, you might think that people would give it a wide berth and leave it to the elephants, lions, snakes and crocodiles. If human beings did live in the midst of such dangerous surroundings you would expect them to be giants, or some kind of a race of supermen, who would be strong enough to defend themselves against the monsters of the jungle.

But many Africans whose home is in this vast wilderness are little people who grow to a height of only four and a half feet and who weigh less than a hundred pounds. And what unusual weapons do they use for their defense against the wild beasts and poisonous snakes of the jungle? Usually only a small spear, a bow and arrow, and nets made from vines that hang from the branches of the trees. Yet with such simple, primitive weapons, they are able to survive, some of them living to be eighty or ninety years of age.

These are the Pygmies, some of the most primitive of the African tribes. Most of them live in the African Congo Basin, but they are also found near the Uganda border in the Ituri Forest, to the north and east near Bahr el Ghazel and west in what was formerly known as French Equatorial Africa.

The iron spear points and arrowheads which the Pygmies use for hunting wild game are obtained by trading with more advanced natives who mine the ore and hammer out the steel on primitive forges. In the mountainous country of Rwanda, which lies on the eastern border of the Congo adjoining Lake Kivu, there are mines of iron ore. By heating the ore over charcoal fires, the natives in this area extract the iron that is used to make the cooking pots, spear points, arrowheads and bush knives upon which they depend for their very existence.

Medicines from Poison Arrows

The bows of the Pygmies are made of tree branches, with a kind of vine, or creeper for the cord. The arrow bow is a reed with a feather attached to one end and the spear point to the other. Yet these simple weapons are very deadly for the arrows and spear points are dipped in poison.

For many years after the white man came to the Congo, this strange poison was a carefully guarded secret. It was finally discovered that one type of arrow poison is made from a species of black ant that is crushed and dried and made into powder. Another poison is obtained from a swamp orchid that grows to a height of five feet, with beautiful purple and red blossoms. The root of this plant is rubbed over the arrows; then there is applied the juice of a yellowish fruit which grows from a shrub called the ounitugunda.

TRUE TALES To Live By

This strange poison has the power to kill an animal within seconds by causing the heart to stop beating. But the flesh can still be used for food. The poison can be swallowed without any harmful effects but if it enters the blood through a deep cut, it will kill almost instantly. For that reason, the Pygmy hunters must use extreme caution in the use of this *poison juice*. If they are wounded by their own spears or arrows, serious illness or death will result.

In some parts of Africa, this substance is gathered and exported to other countries for use as a medicine. It has been found to be very effective in the treatment of certain kinds of heart disease. The National Heart Institute, which has been doing a great deal of research in the medical use of African herbs and plants, reported that a drug know as strophanthidin has been found to reduce the danger of heart failure during surgery. It comes from the same source as an African arrow poison.

The distinguished botanist, John Purseglove, has collected over one thousand plants used by Pygmies and other African natives. These plants are used as poisons, medicines, and in various rituals. They have been proven effective in the treatment of head colds, toothache, malaria and pneumonia. It's amazing to know that these little people, who hunt with spears and bows and arrows and live in tiny huts made of sticks and mud, are playing a part in helping to cure the diseases of civilized society. This fact helps us to realize that the elf-like Pygmies are, in a real sense, our friends.

While the spears and bows and arrows of the Pygmies are effective against certain kinds of animals, such as the monkey, the antelope, and even the gorilla, there are other wild beasts that are a real threat to the safety of the little people, especially at night. The cunning leopard is one of these. He prowls around their camps in the darkness, watching for an opportunity to pounce upon a sleeping victim. But the resourceful Pygmies have two methods of protection from the fierce jungle cat—fire and traps. They always keep a fire burning at night, for the leopard fears the fire. In the Pygmy village, nooses and cleverly disguised traps are placed to catch the unsuspecting leopard. The traps usually consist of deep holes covered with sticks and leaves. Many of these holes have been dug by the Pygmies' fathers or grandfathers but the Pygmies are constantly at work digging new ones, covering them with mongongo leaves, clods of moss, and manure so that even the cunning leopard does not suspect the danger. When an animal falls into this trap, it doesn't take long for the spears and arrows of the hunter to finish him off.

The leopard is the pygmies' most dreaded enemy.

It is foolhardy to travel by foot in Pygmy country without a guide. No matter how cautious you might be, these wild animal traps are so cleverly camouflaged that, —before you realize what has happened, the ground might have given away under your feet and you find yourself in the bottom of a pit. Or you might step into one of the cleverly laid snares that suddenly grabs you about the ankle like a cowboy's lasso. The next moment you find yourself dangling by your feet, high in the air. It would no doubt be an exciting experience but not a very pleasant one.

A hunter once described how a Pygmy could kill an elephant on which he depends for food. The meat is a great delicacy to the little people of the forest. Some of them now use guns on elephant hunts, but the spear is still a favorite weapon among some of the Pygmy tribes.

Trailing these huge beasts requires a great deal of courage and cunning. Sometimes a brave hunter will go out alone on the trail of an elephant. The best way to spot an elephant herd is to climb a tall tree where the view is not obstructed by bushes and vines. When the hunter sights his prey, he takes some bark from the tree, rubs it in his hands to make a powder, and then lets it fall to determine the direction of the wind.

The elephant has poor eyesight but a keen sense of smell and hearing, so the hunter knows he must approach his prey with the wind in his face.

The trained hunter is able to walk so quietly that he can sneak up to within a few feet of the elephant without being detected. Now the time has come to strike. The little man's brow is wet with sweat and his heart is thumping wildly for even the bravest of these daring elephant hunters feels the blood freezing in his veins when he finds himself within a few paces of this giant beast, towering like a mountain above him. He knows that one blow of the elephant's mighty trunk could kill him instantly. He is well aware that if he should be trampled upon by one of those huge feet, it could crush every bone in his body.

Gripping his spear in one hand, the hunter creeps cautiously toward the elephant. Suddenly, he leaps forward until he is directly beneath the beast's stomach. With one quick thrust, he plunges the spear into the elephant's belly. There is a great burst of gas through the wound made by the spear, like a sudden gust of wind. The smell is so sickening that the hunter would faint if he didn't make a quick get-away.

A hunter who had come upon a group of Pygmies who had just killed an elephant related the following story. The elated Pygmies staged a dance around the elephant, then began the task of cutting the meat. Suddenly, with very little warning, a thunderstorm broke loose, pelting down rain in such sheets that the elephant was completely obscured. When the rain stopped and the sun began to break through the green foliage overhead, the hunter was puzzled to observe that the Pygmy hunters had all disappeared. Then, in amazement, he watched the little men emerging from the body of the elephant. One by one, they jumped out of the hole that had been slashed in the animal's belly where they had taken refuge from the storm! They weren't exactly dry, for their bodies, their hair and their beards were smeared with blood, but that didn't seem to concern them in the least.

I feel sad to think that elephant that may have lived for seventy-five years had to be killed. I love the wild creatures of the jungle, and I regret to see them slaughtered.

Those who have lived among these little people of the forest say that they have such an aversion to water that they never take baths or even wash their hands. So one can understand why they avoid wading through streams or rivers. But there is another reason for their avoiding the water—crocodiles! When they find it necessary to cross a stream, they either build a bridge of stout lianas and tree branches, or make swings like jungle Tarzans. To make a swing, they tie and twist several lianas together to make a stout rope. This rope is attached to the branch of a tree at the edge of the stream. Then they make a loop at the bottom end for a seat and a Pygmy climbs into it. Another rope of vines is attached to the seat and strung over the branch of a nearby tree. Several men pull on the rope and raise the little man high in the air. Then they cut the rope and the man sitting in the loop flies through the air like a trapeze performer, down toward the river where the crocodiles snap their jaws in hungry anticipation. But the little fellow swings over their heads beyond their reach and up into the air toward the trees on the opposite shore. Quickly he grasps hold of the branch of a tree, slips out of his seat and makes the swing fast. Then he finds some heavy object, which he fastens to the seat, and he gives the swing a push, sending it back for the next passenger.

TRUE TALES To Live By

When it is necessary for the whole tribe to make the crossing, a crude bridge is usually built, but often even the women with babies on their backs go sailing through the air on the liana swings. It sounds like fun, especially when there are several swings going at one time, but when the river is infested with crocodiles, it's a rather dangerous adventure. If the rope of liana branches should break, as it sometimes does, and the rider drops into the river, his chances of escaping the snapping jaws of crocodiles are not very good.

The clothes that are worn by these elf-like creatures of the forest are as simple as their weapons. Usually all they wear is a tiny apron made from the bark of the marumba tree. The bark is boiled repeatedly; then it is beaten with little ivory hammers to make it pliable. From the jungle trees, the women chip pieces of bark of varying colors, some yellow, and some brown. Their *dress-up* clothes consist merely of several broad green leaves tucked under the back of a cord tied about the waist. They stick out behind like a rooster's tail feathers. Some of the men wear wire bracelets and often they carry, in addition to the spear and the bow and quiver of arrows, a small trumpet made from an elephant's tusk. Their hats, when they wear hats, are tiny ones made of straw or small pieces of hide and decorated with many colored feathers.

The woman's dress is similar to that of the man except that she likes to decorate her little *apron* with various paints or dyes. She carries huge loads on her back, holding the bundle in place with a cord that passes across the forehead and around the bundle. The bundle may contain wood for fuel or food for her family. If she has a baby, it sits on top of the load on her back.

The homes of the Pygmies are as simple as their clothes. They vary in different tribes but generally are constructed in this manner. Long branches are stuck in the ground and then bent together and interwoven to form what resembles the old type of beehive, round on top. Large leaves are fastened to this network of twigs to keep out the rain. This simple hut is not more than three or four feet high at the center. At one side is a tiny hole that serves as a doorway. The little home in the wilderness is furnished with a bed made of leaves.

Their musical instruments consist of flutes, horns, drums, and the *likembe*, a small box-like instrument with vibrating strips of steel. The likembe, which is played with the thumbs, has a beautiful tinkling sound and is a popular instrument with the Pygmies.

Pygmy camps are only temporary. Like bands of gypsies, the little people are continually on the move in search of new hunting grounds. For that reason, few of them plant gardens. Most of their food is obtained from the forest. The men spend most of their time hunting. If their luck is good, they have a variety of meat dishes to enjoy: elephant stew, fried monkey, and occasionally roast gorilla. (Some tribes will not eat the gorilla for they believe it would bring bad luck; others have no scruples about it, and find the meat very tasty.) Other creatures upon which the Pygmies depend for food are the antelope, buffalo, wild pig, baboon and various species of snakes. They also like ants, beetles and many kinds of worms.

Besides the meat of wild animals, the Pygmy enjoys many kinds of fruit, nuts, mushrooms and herbs. He is especially fond of honey and he is so agile and surefooted that he will not hesitate to climb a sixty or seventy-foot tree to rob a bees' nest. As glass jars or cups are not available, the leaves of the mongongo tree are commonly used as a receptacle for the honey, and they seem to serve that purpose very well.

With meat as their main food, you may wonder what these wilderness gypsies eat for dessert. One of their favorite delicacies is roast caterpillars! They wrap the squirming, fuzzy worms in leaves and roast them slowly over a charcoal fire; then they are dropped in a kettle of boiling palm oil. When ready to eat, they resemble shrimp, and the Pygmies love them!

TRUE TALES To Live By

Little Children of the Forest

The Pygmies have often been referred to as *children of the forest*, and the name fits them very well. They look like children because of their small stature. They love to shoot with the bow and arrows as all children do. They get great pleasure from climbing trees and swinging from the branches on their liana swings. Their huts look more like play houses than homes. And like most of the children of the world, they are happy. Scientists who have lived with them and studied their way of life agree that they are among the happiest people in the world, despite the uncertainty of their daily existence.

Pygmies and all African children love animals. Goats are their favorite pets.

Those who have accompanied these primitive people on journeys through the forest are amazed at their endurance. It is not unusual for them to travel on foot all day long (the women with tremendous loads on their backs) then make camp, eat supper, and dance for hours far into the night. White people who have lived among them for years report they have never seen a man or woman die of a heart attack, nor have they seen cases of high blood pressure or ulcers. Yet these people do suffer from disease. In fact, there are many terrifying diseases in the equatorial jungle. There is the yaws, a very contagious disease

110

characterized by horrible sores that sometimes lead to blindness. There is elephantiasis, a disease that is very common in the tropics. It causes a swelling of the limbs and various parts of the body to several times their original size. The natives in this part of Africa also suffer a great deal from influenza, pneumonia and tuberculosis. One of the most serious of all the diseases is the dreaded leprosy that was brought into The Congo many years ago by the Arab slave traders.

Few people made much of an effort to minister to these children of the forest until Dr. Mark Poole, the son of a Texas cattleman, came to the Congo. For many years, he was the only doctor for thousands of the people of the Bakuba tribe who lived in the jungles surrounding the little town of Bulape. (The Bakubas are not Pygmies.) Every day, for months at a time, he examined and treated over one hundred patients, often reaching their villages in a dugout canoe.

His wife, who is a registered nurse, accompanied him on his trips into the bush country. She assisted him in the operating room and in the giving of anesthesia and helped in the work wherever she was needed.

Pygmies Build Airport in the Jungle

Traveling up the rivers and over the rough jungle trails consumed so much of their time that the Pooles finally decided to make use of an airplane. The people of the Shenandoah Presbyterian Church of Miami, Florida, offered to buy a plane for this purpose if a landing field could be built. The construction of an airstrip at Bulape presented a tremendous challenge due to the dense forest that had to be cleared. It took four years to complete the job.

The government of the Congo had an emergency airfield near the village of Bambuya and there Dr. Poole set up his first clinic. Deep in the jungle, seventy miles from

TRUE TALES To Live By

Bambuya, lived the Batua Tribe of Pygmies. When they heard of the good doctor with his *ndeka* (their word for big bird), they built their own landing field.

That, in itself, was an amazing accomplishment, for the Pygmies had no tractors or bulldozers. In fact, they didn't even have shovels or wheelbarrows. These little people went to work with knives and chopped down the bushes; then they dug in the ground with sticks and carried dirt in small buckets to fill up the holes. The only way they knew to pack the ground was with their feet. So they called the drummers together and for several weeks the Pygmies of the surrounding villages danced on the soft earth to make it firm enough for a plane to land. Day after day, often far into the night, there arose from the jungle the sound of laughter and singing and the soft beat of hundreds of little feet.

At last the airstrip was ready for the ndeka to land. You can imagine how the busy people sang and danced for joy on the day the beautiful *big bird* came flying in over the treetops at Batua and landed at the new airfield.

Since that day, the flying doctor and his wife have been making regular trips into Pygmy land. In addition to the Batua airstrip, another was established at Shongomba about seventy-five miles away. They now have three airfields and three air dispensaries scattered over a five thousand square mile area. Each dispensary has a resident medical staff and a local evangelist and a teacher nearby.

The Pooles found the people to be in desperate need of help. Many of them were suffering from sleeping sickness, elephantiasis, and the numerous intestinal diseases of the jungle country. Worst of all, there were literally hundreds of children who were dying from a type of malaria which affects the brain and is one of the most dreaded diseases of the tropics. Dr. Poole's task was not only to treat the people for these diseases but also to educate them in ways of preventing them.

In addition to diseases, there were many injuries for which the Pygmies needed a doctor. They live dangerously.

It is not unusual for a man, woman, or even a little child, to be brought to the hospital in Pygmy country with his flesh torn and bleeding from the clawing of a leopard. Some Pygmies are wounded by the tusks of elephants. In fact, I talked with a man in the Congo who had an elephant tusk run right through his chest; yet recovered after being treated by a mission doctor.

Some of the worst cases Dr. Poole has to treat are patients who have been bitten by crocodiles. Some have lost arms or legs to the attacks of these ferocious reptiles. Of this you can be sure, the people in Pygmy land have little opportunity to become bored with their existence. Adventure lurks around every bend in their paths. The story of this wonderful work that is being done by this dedicated Christian doctor is all the more amazing when you learn that before leaving for the mission field in Africa, Dr. Poole was suffering from a serious heart condition. In fact, his doctor informed him that if he persisted in his plan to go to Africa as a medical missionary, he would die there within a few months. When I visited Bulape, Dr. Poole had been in the Congo for over twenty years and he was still carrying on his medical ministry to the people in this African wilderness.

A Beggar Girl on the Streets of Cairo

About eleven o'clock one night in Cairo, I was taking a brief stroll before retiring to my hotel room when I was accosted by a man who had postcards to sell. Like most of these street peddlers in Cairo who make such a nuisance of themselves, this fellow hung on like a leech, following me for several blocks pleading with me to buy some of his cheap postcards.

As we made our way down the street, I noticed a little girl following a few steps behind. Evidently she was waiting her turn to try her luck as soon as the man made his sale or became discouraged.

TRUE TALES To Live By

Finally I got rid of the fellow but I was so disgusted with him that I didn't even look at the child who had now started in to plead for "just one piastre." I had been told that the police frown on the practice of encouraging these little beggars so I had resolved that I wouldn't give her anything.

As I turned the corner toward my hotel, I glanced at the youngster to tell her that I wasn't going to give her any money. But when I saw her face, my resolution vanished. She was one of the prettiest little girls I had ever seen, with beautiful dark eyes and a sweet smile that went right to your heart. Not more than seven or eight years of age, she wore a shabby red shawl over her hair, and her long native dress almost hid the brown bare feet which appeared and disappeared with each step she took.

I stood for a moment looking down at the sweet, upturned face wondering why the parents of a girl so little and so pretty would permit her to wander about the streets at this hour of the night. Perhaps she had no father or mother.

Suddenly the little girl, with a shy smile, slipped her hand into mine, and that friendly gesture disarmed me completely. I just couldn't resist putting a coin into her hand. As I did so, I noticed a man standing nearby watching me with a sympathetic smile.

I said, "This little girl should be home and in bed at this hour of the night!"

"She has no home," the man replied. "She probably sleeps in the street. There are many like her in Cairo."

The next day I called on a sociology professor in one of the colleges in Cairo to ask about these child beggars. He admitted that what the man on the street had said was true, that in spite of attempts by the government to correct the situation, there were still many homeless children begging on the streets. Many of them, he said, have been sold by their parents to professional beggars and have no place they can call home.

It is sad to realize that there is a place in the world where little children, without the love of a father and a mother, must live under such unhappy conditions, making their beds on door steps or on the hard sidewalk in some back alley. In this city, in the land of the pyramids, there are so many children who have so little—unfortunate waifs who must beg for every crust of bread they have to eat.

Teachers and social workers with whom I talked in Cairo about this problem indicated that there are two main reasons for the sad plight of these homeless children. One is the miserable poverty of so many of the Egyptian people. A large percentage of the parents of these children simply don't have the money with which to buy food for their families, and the offer of the professional beggar is a big temptation to them.

Another factor contributing to this condition is the practice of polygamy that is still widely followed by many of the people in this part of the world. When a man who already has two or three wives takes unto himself another, often the new wife refuses to accept the children of his former marriages. Sometimes she lays down an ultimatum and refuses to allow them in the house. Often they are cruelly mistreated and, in desperation, they run away from home and become easy prey to the unscrupulous professional beggars of the underworld.

One wonders how much worse this distressing situation would be had it not been for the activities of the Christian church in providing orphanages for the homeless children in North Africa. Many thousands of people have played an important part in helping to provide food and clothing for these needy children. The contributions they have made to this worthy project have returned to them many fold in the realization of the suffering they have alleviated.

In the following lines, the poet John Masefield tells what happens when a kindness is done to little children:

"He who gives a child a treat
Makes joybells ring in Heaven's street,
And he who gives a child a home
Builds palaces in Kingdom Come."

TRUE TALES To Live By

Hitchhiking a Ride on a Camel

I traveled several thousand miles by hitchhiking in my college days, when it was still considered legal. Once on my way to Boston, a distance of fifteen hundred miles, I decided I would see how little I could get by with spending on the trip. By sleeping in a haystack one night and depending on the generosity of traveling salesmen who always invited me to eat with them in restaurants along the way, I made the trip of fifteen hundred miles on fifteen cents. All I spent was ten cents for a streetcar fare in Pittsburgh and five cents for subway fare across New York City.

On one of my overseas trips, I continued traveling by hitchhiking. One of the interesting experiences of a traveler in the Middle East is to see camels working in the fields and carrying burdens as they did centuries ago. You can see them in Turkey, on the road from Tarsus to Antioch, and in Israel, as you travel to the Dead Sea from Jericho. There is a camel market in Hebron where camels are bought and sold almost every day of the week. The largest camel market I have ever seen was in Cairo where over one thousand camels were for sale. I talked with a camel driver who had just come in from the desert with a small herd of camels after a journey of over a month.

As one travels through the desert country that borders the Dead Sea, it is fascinating to try to picture the huge caravans that once moved through that bleak wilderness. Bandits often hid in the caves and behind the huge rocks, and for protection from thieves and marauders, travelers were forced to depend on each other. Caravans were known to consist of over five thousand camels and to extend over several miles. In Bible times, wealth was often measured by the number of camels a man owned. Job was said to have over six thousand of these *ships of the desert*. In I Chronicles 5:21 we read of a battle in which the Hagrites were defeated by the armies of Reuben, Gad and Manasseh, and the booty included fifty thousand camels.

SKIP WESTPHAL

My most interesting experience with a camel was during a kind of vagabond trip through parts of Morocco. I hitchhiked a ride on a camel on the road from Casablanca to Marrakesh, unaware at the time that all the Arabs in that desolate country carried knives and some would welcome the opportunity to cut a man's throat for a few coins. But I was unaware of the danger so I can't say that it was an act of courage on my part.

At the beginning of the journey, I met an Arab who spoke both French and Arabic and I knew enough French so that he could teach me how to ask for a ride on a camel in Arabic. "Barakalowfik, Sidi, ana housa fog shamel?" means "Greetings, Sir, may I ride on your camel?"

When I left my Arab friend, I continued on foot along the road to Marrakesh. After an hour or so I met a camel driver riding a donkey and driving a lone camel. I accosted him with the Arabic expression and he reluctantly had the camel get down for me to mount him.

First the camel got up on his front knees and I almost slipped off on his tail. Then he stood up on his back legs and I almost slid over his head. It was an interesting ride until he began to trot; then it almost shook my teeth loose. I rode along for several miles and I was relieved when the driver left the main road for a village in the mountains and I continued on my way on foot toward Marrakesh.

New adventures are always challenging but one experience I think I could do without would be traveling for several days on the back of a camel. I am sure that reading about it would be much more fun.

A Meeting with a Puff Adder

On my last journey through Africa, I not only heard many amazing stories about snakes but I had a very unpleasant encounter with one. One dark night I was making my way across a camp where I was staying in the Hluhluhwe Game

TRUE TALES To Live By

Reserve when suddenly something struck me hard, like the blow of a hammer, on the calf of my right leg. I could not see what had struck me because of the darkness but I knew I had been bitten by a snake. I called for help and a friend rushed me to the home of the game warden's mother, about a quarter of a mile away. She administered the snake bite serum but there had been a lapse of twenty to twenty-five minutes between the time of the bite and the serum injection. The next morning I was able to hobble about with the aid of a cane and managed to get to a doctor in the nearest village, about thirty miles distant.

The doctor examined my swollen leg and remarked, "If you could have had that serum injection about ten minutes sooner, you wouldn't have had all this trouble." Then he added with a grin, "If you had gotten it ten minutes later, you wouldn't have had this trouble either!" I can't say that I appreciated his sense of humor.

After about ten days, a blood clot developed in the leg, and I spent about two weeks in bed. A month later, I suffered an attack of phlebitis and had to spend ten days in a hospital in the Argentine. In all, it was a long, drawn out, unhappy experience.

This unpleasant experience with a poisonous snake led me to make a study of the reptiles that almost everyone seems to despise. One day I visited the world famous Snake Park in Durban, South Africa. The owner of the snake pits, Mr. Fitzsimmons, gave me some startling information regarding the important contribution poisonous snakes are making to medical science. He reported that he removes the venom from the puff adder, (which was probably the snake I had the argument with in the Hluhluhwe Game Reserve.) He supplies this snake poison to pharmaceutical factories all over the world for the purpose of making a drug that is used very effectively in the treatment of epilepsy. He also reported that the venom from the deadly cobra is used in a drug that relieves the pain of cancer when other drugs have lost their effectiveness. Another snake, the Russell's viper, which is found in India and Ceylon, also provides materials for drug manufacturers. Its venom, when mixed in a salt solution of one to ten thousand, is effective in preventing bleeding. Dentists are indebted to this snake for its contribution to the making of a drug known as stypven, which is used as a coagulant.

How many of us realize that when we sit in a dentist's chair, one of the dentist's assistants may be a deadly snake from Ceylon? Mr. Fitzsimmons expressed the opinion that in years to come more and more use will be made of snake venom for medicinal purposes, especially in the treatment of mental illness. In view of these facts, how can we look with disdain on any creature God has made?

Chased by a Lion

Central Congo is a part of Africa where adventure seems to lurk around every bend of the road. Burleigh Law, one of the staff at the Wembo Nyama Mission, shot a man-eating lion in the wooded area surrounding the village. One of the African pastors, Ngondjolo Mose, had the unpleasant experience of being chased by a lion one day.

He was riding his motorcycle along a path through the woods when suddenly a lion leaped at him from the bushes along the roadside. But the lion misjudged the speed of the motorcycle...and missed. The frightened pastor looked over his shoulder and saw that the lion was giving chase, stirring up a cloud of dust as he galloped up the road only a few yards behind him.

Pastor Mose turned the throttle up to full speed, his heart in his throat for fear that the motorcycle might break down and leave him at the mercy of the lion. He was always having trouble with the spark plugs fouling up and if that should happen now, Mose would be in for serious trouble.

But fortunately, the spark plugs kept firing and the lion was finally left behind in a cloud of dust. They say

TRUE TALES To Live By

when pastor Mose reached the next village, his eyes were like saucers and he was actually pale with fright.

It was very fortunate for the people of the Congo that the lion wasn't able to catch up with the motorcycle that day for Ngondjolo Mose was the leader of a revival movement that was then sweeping the Congo. For three years, he had been the central figure in an amazing religious awakening among the people of central Africa. His open-air services were being attended by as many as five to six thousand people each, and at one gathering, over a thousand people made decisions for the Christian life. It was not unusual for people to walk as far as fifty miles to hear Ngondjolo Mose preach.

When I arrived in the Lodja area where these meetings were being held, the people were still talking about a service where four converts confessed to cannibalism and one man admitted that he had killed and eaten twenty-four human beings.

Methodist missionary Alexander J. Reid, who attended the service, told about a two hour session of testimonies that followed one Friday night meeting. As one man got up, whispers could be heard throughout a large part of the congregation. According to Reid, this is roughly what he said:

> For the past fifteen years, I have had an insatiable hunger for eating human flesh. I have killed and eaten about twenty-four people during this period of time. But during this revival, God has clearly shown me the awfulness of my sin and I have come to him confessing it and asking Him to give me a new heart. I believe He has done it and He has delivered me. I want you all to know it and to pray for me!

This story does not indicate, of course, that cannibalism is sweeping the Congo! But there are some isolated areas where this heathen custom is still being practiced.

120

SKIP WESTPHAL

I met Ngondjolo Mose at Lodja one night as I was about to board a plane for Luluabourg. I asked him what he considered to be the reason for the success of the revival movement in the Lodja area. His reply was simple and to the point. "It has been due," he said, "to fasting and prayer."

On returning home, I often told this story in my lectures on Africa. At my first presentation, I inadvertently said, "A friend of mine in Africa had a frightening experience one day. He was chased by a lion on a motorcycle." The audience roared with laughter. Then with a grin of embarrassment I corrected my remark by explaining, "What I meant to say that my friend was riding his motorcycle one day when he was chased by a lion."

After that embarrassing experience, when I gave my African lecture, I repeated my story about the lion on the motorcycle just to get a laugh from my audience.

A Call on the King of the Bakubas

I have had the privilege of meeting two presidents of the United States, Dwight Eisenhower and Jimmy Carter, but I hadn't ever met a king until I made a trip to Africa. I was traveling with a missionary on my way to the copper mines of Katanga. He had met Lukengo Bope Mabintsi, king of the Bakubas, whose palace was located near Bulape, and he thought he might arrange an audience for me.

I tried to imagine what the palace of an African king would look like. I was surprised, when we arrived, to discover that his palace had the appearance of a huge grass hut. My friend entered the unguarded door to see if we could get an appointment. In a few minutes, he emerged to announce that the king would be happy to see me.

When the king appeared, he was followed by five members of his council of ministers. I expected that his majesty might be dressed in a robe or some kind of attire

121

befitting a king, but he wore only a dress that hung low over his hips.

The king spoke English, and in our brief conversation I asked if we could meet the queen. He informed me that he had two hundred and eighty wives. He said he once had many more, but some of them had died.

I was surprised when he offered to have some of them stage a dance for me.

I found it interesting that, in our brief meeting, he didn't tell me he was proud of the accomplishments of his tribe.

When we left the palace, my friend informed me that the Bakuba tribe is famous all over the world for their sculpture and crafts which were considered to be among the finest in Africa. I wish the king had taken me on a tour of his palace so I could see some of the artistic work of his people.

The King of the Bakubas and his Council of Ministers.

SKIP WESTPHAL

Black Mamba Captures Thief

Every day the newspapers carry stories of people who are reaping the harvest of their wrongdoing. While these stories are depressing they serve a useful purpose in that they illustrate the truth of the quotation from Numbers 32:23:"Be sure your sin will find you out."

One of the most dramatic stories I have ever heard which illustrates this fact was told to me several years ago during one of the trips through the diamond mining country of South Africa. Two partners had been working together for several years along the river beds in western South Africa, prospecting for diamonds. All their efforts, however, had netted them only a few small stones, not enough to pay even for their food.

Then one day as they were laboriously sifting out the gravel on a riverbank, a sparkle in the sand caught the eye of one of the prospectors. It was a diamond—one of the largest he had ever seen. He estimated that it might be worth at least a hundred thousand dollars! The other partner had not seen it. Although the men had made an agreement to share and share alike this was too much of a temptation for the finder of the stone to resist. He resolved to say nothing about his discovery; then he would have the entire fortune for himself

That night after supper by the campfire, the lucky prospector crawled into his blanket, feigning illness. Patiently he waited until his partner had fallen asleep; then he stealthily slipped out of camp clutching the precious stone in his shirt pocket.

The next morning when the man by the riverbank awoke, his partner was nowhere to be seen. When he called out and received no reply, he began to search the area and discovered his tracks in the sand. For several hours, the prospector followed the footprints across a desert area becoming increasingly suspicious of his friend's sudden desertion.

123

Finally he came to the banks of a small stream. There beside a bush were the smoking ashes of a campfire, and a short distance away lay the body of his former partner. The man was dead. One hand was tightly closed. When the prospector pried open the dead man's hand, there in his palm, lay the beautiful diamond. In the bushes partly hidden by a small rock was something else—a Black Mamba, the most deadly of Africa's poisonous snakes whose bite will kill it's victim within five minutes. The snake, too, was dead. Evidently the mamba had bitten the man and he had the strength to kill the snake before the poison killed him. Is it necessary to point out the moral of the story?

What Africans Can Teach Us

We who live in a civilized society may wonder if there is anything we can learn from a primitive African who lives in a grass hut, sleeps on the dirt floor and hunts with a spear or a bow and arrow. Yet even a brief study of his way of life leads us to the conclusion that there is a great deal he can teach us.

One of the characteristics of the people of Africa for which I have always had a great deal of admiration is the way they love to sing at their work. No matter how difficult their task or how hot and uncomfortable the weather, it is very seldom that they don't have a song on their lips to make their burden lighter.

I recall on one occasion at the Port of Mombasa in Kenya. I had gone down to the docks to get some pictures of the dockhands unloading the boats. Climbing painfully up the steps to the waterfront was an old man who looked as if he were at least seventy years of age. On his back he carried a huge bundle of poles, so heavy that he staggered under their weight. But he sang a song as he climbed those stairs. On each step, he would pause for a moment to do a bit of a chant; then he would take another step and do another little chant, and so it went, all the way to the top of the steps. I am sure that his cheerful song made his burden seem a little bit lighter.

I told this story one day to a friend, Miss Margaret Moore, who is serving with the Salvation Army as a foreign mission outpost teacher in Nigeria. She mentioned another characteristic of the African people is their attitude about the things they can't change. They are not fatalists, as we use the term, but they seem to have learned how to put needless worry from their minds. Miss Moore tells a delightful story to illustrate this point.

"One day," she said, "I was summoned to the Calabar court with instructions to be present by ten o'clock. Getting there involved a trip by car to Oron, and from there, a two-hour trip by launch.

"The first launch was due to leave Oron at eight o'clock, and well before that time, I was waiting at the pier. All around me were Nigerians waiting to go to Calabar. Some had their children. Some had heavy loads for sale at the market.

"Just before eight o'clock, an official appeared to announce that there would be no early launch. We would have to wait for the 10:30 boat. I walked about impatiently, shoving my hands in my pockets and getting indigestion at the thought of the delay.

"All about me the crowd was at ease...laughing, chatting, even sleeping. The market women whose, profits dwindled with each passing hour, leaned patiently against their loads.

"Finally one woman looked at me and in an amused but kindly tone, she said, 'But Mina, it's a matter of can't help'."

We wonder how many ulcers, nervous breakdowns and heart attacks we Americans could avoid if we had that kind of patience and could learn how to laugh more at ourselves, especially when our troubles aren't too serious. Most of the people of Africa have never heard of William

TRUE TALES To Live By

Shakespeare, but they know what he was talking about when he said, "What's gone and what's past help should be past grief."

Apollo Mweja

In my travels in Africa, I have met many interesting people. The Pygmies who have survived in a jungle inhabited by many ferocious animals, a man who barely escaped an attack by a lion and later led many cannibals to the Lord, and Lukengo Bope Mabinishi, king of the Bakubas with his 180 wives.

But the man whose life is a real miracle is an African by the name of Apollo Mweja. There was a time when Apollo Mweja was considered one of the most dangerous criminals in the southern Congo. He was known to the police in the mining town of Kolwezi as a troublemaker of the worst sort.

Thrown into jail for disturbing the peace during a drunken brawl, Apollo Mweja soon got the reputation of having the worst temper of any man ever imprisoned in the Kolwezi jail. One day in a fit of rage, he struck a fellow prisoner over the head with a club and killed him. While awaiting trial for that crime, he was put into chains with his hands tightly bound behind his back. Because of his insolent manner and his uncontrollable temper, he was often beaten by the prison guards. He still bears the scars from the chains and the beatings he received. The man was considered to be completely incorrigible.

Following his conviction for the murder of his fellow inmate, Mweja was transferred to the government prison at Elizabethville. In the evenings, after the day's work was through, he shared his chains in his prison cell with another convicted murderer, Simon Mutombo, who had once attended church at the Presbyterian Mission in Luebo.

SKIP WESTPHAL

Mutombo subscribed to the mission's monthly paper known as the *Luma Lua Bena Kasai,* meaning, news of the people of the Kasai. As this was the only reading material they had, the two men read the little magazine from cover to cover every month. Over and over they read the stories of how the lives of people were being changed through the influence of the Christian church. Mutombo had no Bible but he knew by heart many verses that he had memorized as a part of his early schooling. Sitting there with chains about their wrists, in the darkness of the prison cell, Mutombo would repeat those Bible verses to his cell mate and the two men would talk about the meaning of the words of Jesus. As Mweja later described it, "Even before I saw or read a Bible, the message of God's Word found its way through prison bars, from one murderer's lips into another murderer's heart."

Slowly, a miracle began to take place in the life of Apollo Mweja. There began to grow within his heart a great longing to find something of the peace and the joy which real faith in God could bring.

At the end of ten months, Mweja's friend was transferred to another prison, but the seed had been planted. Through friends, he was able to acquire a Bible from a Methodist missionary in Elizabethville. During the day, he would carry it under his prison pullover and every night, by the light of a small lamp, he read from it. One passage, he said, "gripped my heart with a band of steel." It was the seventh verse of the 146th Psalm which reads "The Lord looseth the prisoners." Is it possible, he wondered, that this God about whom he was learning, could so change circumstances that he, a prisoner under life sentence, could be set free?

One night as he sat in his cell, reading his Bible by the flickering lamp light, he came to the story of Saul in the book of Acts. When he read that story, the presence of Jesus seemed to come right through the prison walls. He felt that he, like Saul, had been kicking against the pricks all his life.

TRUE TALES To Live By

It was then he resolved if the Lord would release him from prison, he would give the rest of his life to God's service.

The change that came about in the life of this prisoner soon became apparent to the prison guards, and Mweja was made *kaput*, or head prisoner with supervisory responsibilities. His experience with God began to mean so much to him that he felt he must share it with his fellow prisoners, and he began to preach to them in little informal groups whenever he had the opportunity.

After several years of good behavior, Mweja was given an unconditional release from prison. The conclusion of that story is that today Apollo Mweja is in charge of a group of sixty first- grade children in a School at Port Franqui. He is one of the best teachers the school has ever had. In addition to performing his teaching duties, he is studying for the Christian ministry.

In relating this story, one of my missionary friends, Mrs. Miller, said to me, "That man is now one of the gentlest souls you could ever hope to meet. He's a big giant of a man, six feet seven inches tall, and the boys and girls in his school idolize him. The terrible temper that had driven him to murder is completely gone and he has become a Christian gentleman in the truest sense of the word.

Mooney, the Pet Lion

In my description of Africa's wild life, I have pictured the animals as ferocious and to be feared. I will now tell a story about some of the lions in Africa which are not only loveable but also gentle and have a feeling of affection for those who are kind to them.

On my first trip to Africa, I wasn't interested in going on a hunting safari where the object was to kill a lion. I had worked in a circus where I had learned to love the wild animals and it was unthinkable for me to make a trip to Africa for the purpose of killing one of God's creatures.

SKIP WESTPHAL

One day I arrived in Nairobi, Kenya, armed not with a gun but with a camera. I found it easy to get pictures of antelopes or giraffe but my hope was to bring back home pictures of a wild lion. I had no success. What frustrated me was that several times travelers in a car only minutes behind me reported seeing lions, one with several little cubs, but for some strange reason, the king of the jungle kept eluding me.

One day I met a Norwegian, Bjorn Figenshou. He said, "Come with me. We'll visit the Ngoro Ngoro Crater. There, I promise you, we will see lions like herds of cattle."

We toured the crater the whole day. We saw all kinds of wild life—giraffes, hundreds of zebra and antelope, but not one lion. Once we came upon a baby zebra that my friend guessed wasn't more than a day or two old. Its mother stood protectively nearby. I got a picture of the little fellow, lively and as innocent looking as a baby colt. Although my friend had said we would see lions like herds of cattle, we saw not one lion.

We had an experience that day which was rather frightening! We had just started back toward camp when Figenshou exclaimed, "Look over to the right. Do you see that rhino?"

There he was, the first wild rhino I had ever seen. He was standing very still, almost hidden by the tall grass, looking directly at us. Figenshou stopped the jeep with the car in gear and his foot on the clutch ready to take off if the rhino should decide to charge. Crouching in the back of the jeep, I took three or four shots with my camera, then glanced down to make an adjustment in the lens opening.

At that moment, Figenshou shouted, "Here he comes! Hang on to your hat. We're getting out of here."

As he let in the clutch, he took off with a jerk that threw me off my feet. Looking out of the back window, I saw the rhino charging after us, drawing ever closer as we shifted from low to second to high. The rhino now was within about thirty feet of the car. There was no road and the tall grass hid the holes and the rocks in our path, but there was no choice but to throw caution to the winds and step on the gas.

That was the wildest ride I had ever experienced. Over the rocks and through the holes we went, the jeep lurching from one side to the other with the angry rhino in hot pursuit.

"Are we gaining on him?" Figenshou shouted.

'No," I called back, "he's gaining on us. He's only about ten feet behind. Can't you go any faster?"

I crawled back into the front seat expecting at any moment to feel the rear end of the car rise up in the air. I knew that if the rhino got his horn under the jeep, he could toss it up in the air like a rubber ball. Figenshou looked grim as he gripped the steering wheel, trying to avoid the rocks and the holes that blocked our way.

Suddenly he shouted. "There's a smooth stretch of grass just ahead. If we can reach that, we'll leave him behind."

I looked out of the rear window again and was relieved to see that the rhino was losing ground. Suddenly he stopped, slowly turned and soon disappeared in the tall grass.

"We've lost him," I announced with a feeling of relief.

"Whew!" Figenshou gulped as he wiped his forehead on his sleeve. "That was a little too close for comfort!"

At that moment the jeep came to a sudden stop.

"Why are you stopping now?" I asked. "That rhino isn't too far away. He may come after us again!"

I'm stopping," Figenshou announced "because we're stuck in this mud hole. You'll have to get out and push."

I leaped from the jeep and put my shoulder to the fender, now and then looking back to see if the rhino had seen our predicament and had decided to take advantage of it, but we finally got out of the mud and continued on our way without further mishap.

We had started out that morning with such confidence. When Figenshou had promised that I would see "lions like herds of cattle," I had high hopes that my search would at last be rewarded. Words can't describe my feeling of frustration at the end of that day's trip in the Ngoro Ngoro Crater.

One day later, I had checked into a hotel in Moshi, Tanzania. The next morning, I was about to leave for the hotel dining room when there was a knock at my door. When I opened it, there stood a man and his wife looking very tired. The man, Siegfred Jugl, said that they had to sleep in their car overnight for there was no room at the hotel. They wondered if I was about to check out of my room. I invited them in and during our brief conversation I told them how frustrated I was because I had been unable to get a picture of a lion.

Said Mr. Jugl, "If it would make you feel any better, I'll tell you about my pet lion."

Often I asked the question. "Why did Mr. Jugl climb the stairs and knock at my door?" I have also wondered why I couldn't get a picture of a lion in all of the time I had traveled in Africa, although I did see a lion with cubs several days later. I know the answer. My wonderful Lord had been guiding my steps to make the Mooney story possible. Out of my disappointment came a wonderful experience.

Following is a brief summary of the story as I remember him telling it.

One morning while exploring the woods near his farm home, Mr. Jugl came upon a whimpering lion cub. It had evidently gotten lost from its mother. The cub was frightened at the sight of a stranger but he was too tired to run away. Mr. Jugl looked cautiously in the bushes where he had spotted the little cub. He feared the mother might be nearby and then he would be in trouble. He didn't want to leave the cub out there in the bushes as it would starve without a mother. He finally decided to pick it up and take it home.

When Mr. Jugl reached home, he was greeted by his wife and his son Barrie. They were delighted to see that cute little cub and pestered Mr. Jugl with questions as to how he had found it. They gave it something to eat and then it was decided to make a bed for it in the corner of Jugl's bedroom. He was tired from the day's activities and he crawled into bed and was soon fast asleep. But the cub couldn't sleep. He felt lonely in that strange room. He was not afraid of the man who was so kind to him. He sneaked out of the corner of the room and crawled up on the bed beside his friend. Then he put his head on the pillow and he, too, fell asleep.

When Mr. Jugl awoke in the morning, to his surprise, there was the lion cub with his head on the pillow fast asleep. There was no doubt now that Mooney had found a new home.

One of Mooney's favorite sports was to play ball with Barrie who would throw the ball as Mooney leaped high in the air to catch it.

Mooney's favorite playmates were the other pets in the household—a Dachshund named Oscar and a black Labrador dog. Those animals became the best of friends. Sometimes they would chase each other all around the house, climbing on the tables and upsetting the furniture.

When they became tired, all three of them would lie down in front of the fireplace to take a nap. Usually Oscar would sleep with his chin on Mooney's paw.

There were times when Oscar and Mooney got into arguments at mealtimes. If Mooney looked away from his feeding dish for a moment, Oscar would grab a piece of meat and run off with it. Instead of chasing the little dog, Mooney would set up a howl calling to Mrs. Jugl to help. Then she would chase after Oscar to get back Mooney's food. With his jaws the lion cub could really have hurt that Dachshund but he liked his little friend and he wouldn't ever have done such a thing. What Mooney loved most was riding in the automobile with his master. When he was still only a little cub, he would sit in the front seat with Mr. Jugl. When he became too big for the front seat, he would sit in the back and rest his chin on his master's shoulder as he drove along the countryside on his way to Nairobi.

Until people became accustomed to it, they were startled to see a man driving along the streets with the bushy head of a lion snuggled against his shoulder or peering out of the car window.

The Jugl farm was located near a forest and bush country that was inhabited by lions. They seemed to sense that the people who lived there were friendly to animals. At times when Mr. Jugl came home from the fields and was walking across the yard he passed quite close to several lions lying in the shade of a tree. He had no fear of them and they knew that he was their friend.

As we sat that day in our hotel room, I listened in amazement to the fascinating story of that lion cub. He told how one evening when the family was sitting on the porch enjoying their evening meal, a number of wild lionesses walked in single file right where the family was sitting. They counted them. There were twelve lionesses that probably came to pay a visit to Mooney.

"Do you know what I think?" Mrs. Jugl remarked. "I think Mooney told those lionesses that we were friends and they were not to harm us. They were probably leaving their cubs with one mother lion to babysit with them. They sometimes do that when they are going on a hunt."

Then she told of an experience she sometimes had when she looked out of her kitchen window and could see the lionesses playing in the barnyard. Some would be lying asleep in the shade of the pepper trees. Others would be swatting at butterflies or chasing after owls. Often two or three of them would be dragging around an old hay cart that stood near the corner of the barn.

Then with a smile she added, "They loved to jump up on that hay cart and play on it."

I asked my friends if they still had Mooney on their farm. A sad look came over their faces.

"We finally realized," Mrs. Jugl said, "that you really can't trust a full grown lion. We know Mooney would never attack us, but he attracts the wild lionesses and there is no telling what they might do when they are frightened. It was also getting to be very expensive to feed Mooney. Sometimes he would eat forty-five pounds of meat at one

TRUE TALES To Live By

meal. Since we would be absent for some time at the farm, we finally decided that we would have to part with him. The manager of a zoo in England heard of Mooney and he offered to take care of him at the zoo.

It was a sad day for the Jugl family when their lion was put into a cage and sent away. They were consoled, however, knowing that thousands of children visiting the zoo would enjoy seeing Mooney and hear about his amazing experiences on that African farm.

What Africa Gives To Us

On returning from one of my African trips, I kept busy giving lectures with slides of my experiences.

Marion Hammond, a nurse friend who later became my wife, accompanied me and operated the slide projector. After one of our programs, she offered a suggestion. "Why do you talk so much about cannibalism and the primitive African who lives in a grass hut and hunts with a spear and a bow and arrow? Why don't you tell about the modern African who lives in cities like ours and provides us with many of our modern conveniences?"

I gave that suggestion some serious thought and began to do some research on the subject. I made some amazing discoveries. I agreed that the common modern conception of Africa is that of a strange faraway land populated by Ubangis, poisonous snakes and wild animals. The native African is considered by many to be an uneducated, uncivilized savage who contributes little or nothing to modern society.

The fact is that there are very few people who are not benefited practically every day of their lives by products that come from Africa. The native from faraway Africa plays a significant part in our radio and television programs, for the metal cobalt, over seventy percent of which comes from Africa, is used in the construction of radio and television transmitters. Much of the food on our dining room tables has in it something from Africa, for cobalt is used in feed for sheep, cattle, and hogs, as well as in medicines for the animals which provide us with our pork chops, mutton, beefsteak and hamburgers.

Much of our farm machinery has something of Africa in it. For in one stage of the steel manufacturing process, the sheets of metal are immersed in a bath of palm oil. Most of the world's supply of palm oil comes from Nigeria and the Congo.

The African also plays a part in the manufacture of our automobiles and airplanes. It is he who mines ninety-five percent of the world's supply of industrial diamonds that go into the diamond impregnated tools used in the making of motor parts, especially in the boring of piston pin holes and connecting rod bearings.

The industrial diamond touches many phases of modern life. It goes into the lights that illuminate our homes, as the filaments in electric light bulbs are drawn through diamond dies. The same is true of the tiny wires in radio and television tubes.

Diamond drills are used in making parts for refrigerators, in turning commutators for electric motors, and in boring fountain pen barrels. The industrial diamond is employed by the optician in grinding lenses for eyeglasses, by the dentist in his drills, and by the watch manufacturer in making dies for watch cases.

It is the diamond drills from Africa that bore deep into the earth through layers of rock to reach the reserves of oil we need to keep our automobiles, tractors and airplanes running. Without this oil, our modern machine civilization would grind to a complete stop.

The African is even a silent partner in our love affairs and our marriages, for it is he who mines practically all of the diamonds which go into our engagement rings and most of the gold for our wedding rings.

Another of Africa's contributions to our modern world is evident in the field of medicine. One of the most important contributions is the drug, reserpine which is obtained from the root of the ruwolfia tree. This miracle drug is being used very effectively throughout the world in the treatment of heart trouble and mental illness. Its widest use is in the treatment of mental disease. Patients suffering from schizophrenia, chronic alcoholism and drug addiction have been aided greatly by this mysterious medicine obtained from the root of the rauwolfia tree. This miracle drug is widely used in the treatment of arthritis and various types of skin disease. An ingredient in this drug is stigmasterol that is derived mainly from the soya and Calabar beans. One of the chief sources of supply for the Calabar bean is Nigeria, West Africa.

The metal manganese, which is one of Africa's chief exports, is also of importance to the medical profession. When combined with potassium, it is made into potassium permanganate, a solution that is used as a disinfectant in the treatment of skin diseases.

In the battle against cancer, the continent of Africa is becoming increasingly important. Cobalt cancer clinics, in which radio activated cobalt is used to alleviate pain, are being established throughout the world. Many cases have been reported in which the spread of the disease has been checked with the use of cobalt and, in some instances, the results seem to indicate a complete cure. Since almost three-fourths of the world's supply of cobalt comes from Africa, it can be assumed that the people of that continent who mine the cobalt are playing an important part in the fight against cancer.

Even the despised snakes from the so called *Dark Continent* have a use in medical science. Mr. D. C. Fitzsimmons, of Durban, South Africa, director of one of the world's largest snake parks, reports that snake venom is being used today in the treatment of epilepsy and various types of nervous disorders. From the venom of the cobra, a non-habit forming drug has been developed which relieves the pain of diseases such as cancer when other drugs have lost their effectiveness.

SKIP WESTPHAL

One of the most important of Africa's contributions to medical science has come from her monkeys and chimpanzees. In the laborious task of developing the polio vaccine, it was discovered that the monkey's nervous system was the only tissue outside of the human body in which the polio virus would grow and live, and therefore it was the only animal in which the experimental virus could be tested. It is the opinion of scientists who have done research in this field that had it not been for the part played by monkeys in the experiments, the development of the polio vaccine would have been long delayed. Africa's contribution to the health and happiness of our modern world is no idle phrase when one thinks of the thousands of healthy, happy children who would have been crippled for life had it not been for the monkeys and the chimpanzees from Africa.

Our health and that of our children is dependent in so many ways on the people we have never seen and never will see from that land across the seas. In a very real sense, it is the man from Africa who stands beside the doctor in the sick room with medicines to relieve our pains and cure our diseases.

It is not only with cobalt, gold and diamonds, palm oil and medicines that the African contributes to our happiness and well being. Africa sends us rubber and manganese from Liberia, cocoa from Ghana, perfumes from Algeria and Ethiopia, and spices from Madagascar. These are but a few of the essentials of modern life that come to us from a land that has so much to contribute to our civilization.

The purpose of these stories is to tell something of the exciting story behind these rich contributions Africa is making to the rest of the world. We are not satisfied to know that the people of Africa have contributed to our happiness and well being with medicines, gold, diamond, cobalt, palm oil, cocoa, spices, perfumes and many other important materials. We want to be familiar with the fascinating account of the discovery and development of these products and to know something about the people who provide them for us.

TRUE TALES To Live By

With this background of information about Africa, one day I got a brilliant idea. Why not apply for a grant from the Ford Foundation to finance another trip to Africa to visit the gold, diamonds, and cobalt mines and get more information, first hand, about Africa's contribution to modern life. I would use a sound recorder as well as a camera. I had been promised that on my return, I could run a series of twenty-four radio programs on my experiences in Africa over WOI Radio Station in Ames, Iowa.

I didn't really have much hope that the Ford Foundation, with all its requests, would accept my proposal. Several weeks passed and I had given up on the idea that my request would be granted.

Imagine my surprise when I went to the mailbox one morning and found among the letters an envelope containing a check for thirty-three hundred dollars to finance a trip to Africa!

My plan was to take a river boat trip up the Congo River to Brabanta, where the palm plantations are located, then to the gold mines of Johannesburg and to the area of Kimberly in central Congo to tour the diamond mines.

Perfumes from Africa

I wasted no time booking passage on an ocean liner for Leopoldville in the Congo. On my arrival in New York , since I had a couple of days before leaving for the Congo, and I decided to visit the Fritzche Laboratories. This company is a supplier of the essential oils that are used in perfumes, toiletries and cosmetics.

While on a tour of the plant, my guide told me a story that was almost unbelievable. He took from a shelf a buffalo horn about two feet long with a goatskin tied over the end of it. He removed the goatskin from the buffalo horn. It was almost full of a dark colored substance resembling mud. The smell of the stuff almost made me reel. My guide informed me that this odor, from the foul smelling civet cat, is used in the making of our sweet smelling perfumes.

One wonders how anybody got the idea that such a thing as civet could be used in making perfumes. My guide informed me that the main source of civet is Ethiopia in Northeast Africa where civet cats are raised for the perfume industry.

I was informed that one of the tricks employed by the shippers of the civet had been to mix the precious substance with honey to increase its weight. Before modern methods of discovering this deception were developed, a man was hired to take a taste of a new shipment to determine if it contained any honey! I don't know what his salary was but I am sure he earned it!

As I looked at that buffalo horn the thought occurred to me that it might make an interesting souvenir for my collection of African relics. However, my enthusiasm cooled a bit when the guide told me what had happened to one of the workers in the plant who once had a similar idea. He decided that one of these horns would make a beautiful decoration over the mantelpiece above his fireplace. To get rid of the scent he buried the horn.

Two years later, when he dug it up, he found that the odor still remained. So he put the horn back in the ground. After another two years when it still smelled of civet, he decided to give up the idea.

As we continued our interesting tour of the laboratories my guide showed me another valuable material used in perfumes. It is known as *ambergris*, a rare substance disgorged by sick whales. The most valuable chunk of ambergris ever discovered was found by a New Bedford sea captain about fifty years ago. It was reported to be worth $150,000.

When we think about how such things as civet and ambergris could be used in the making of sweet smelling perfumes to make our charming ladies more alluring we

TRUE TALES To Live By

are reminded of those lines from the pen of Ralph Waldo Emerson:

> 'Tis not in the high stars alone, Nor in the cups of budding flowers, Nor in the red breasts mellow tone, Nor in the bow that shines in showers, But in the mud and scum of things, There always, always something sings.

There are other materials, of course, which are used in the making of perfumes. One of these is the ylang ylang flower that is cultivated principally on the Island of Madagascar off the east coast of Africa.

Another African plant that has an important place in perfume manufacturing is the jasmine flower that is grown in Egypt and Algeria. Women pick the blossoms of the flower and carry it on their heads for miles. At the processing plants, the essence is extracted from the blossoms and used in the most expensive perfumes. It takes many baskets of the jasmine petals to make even one ounce of perfume. At the conclusion of my tour of the Fritzche Plant, my guide took from a shelf a bottle of jasmine absolute. The bottle contained only three ounces of perfume and it was valued at approximately nine thousand dollars.

The more research I did about what Africa contributes to our way of life, the more eager I became for the tour which the Ford Foundation had made possible for me. A few days later I found myself back in Africa.

By Riverboat up the Congo

When my ship docked in Leopoldville, I was told that a road trip through the jungle to Brabanta would be a very long, tiresome journey. A trip by riverboat would be much more desirable. Following is a description of this never-to-be forgotten two-week trip up the Congo River, as described in one of my "True Tales" columns.

SKIP WESTPHAL

My first four weeks in Africa have been hot - miserably hot. But this boat trip up the Congo River is like drifting along through paradise. I have been told that this Congo River trip is often very sticky and hot, but the weatherman has been kind this week, providing enough clouds to cover the sun and sending along those refreshing gentle breezes which provide such a blessed relief from the oppressive heat of Leopoldville.

The scene is always changing. Sometimes you creep along for hours through dense jungle country, deep and dark and forbidding, which you know must be crawling with all manner of poisonous snakes. Then you come to a country of green rolling hills, made especially verdant and beautiful by the soaking rains that have fallen during the past two weeks.

Now and then, as the boat rounds a bend in the river, you see a clearing among the trees, and there, nestled on the river bank, is a village of grass huts. As the boat's long whistle announces its approach, the young men of the village take to their pirogues, or canoes, and come toward the ship. These boatmen paddle their canoes while standing up. One explanation is that a boatman is not in so much danger of having his arm taken off by a crocodile if his hand is not too close to the water.

When the men reach the ship, they paddle alongside and try to latch on to the side of the vessel. This is a rather dangerous operation for the waves caused by the movement of the ship could very easily upset a tiny pirogue unless the boatman is very skillful. It's a sport which might be compared to an attempt to board a moving freight train while on a dead run, except that jumping on a train is probably less likely to end in a spill.

This exciting adventure is not indulged in just for fun. The natives have their pirogues loaded with bananas, manyok, peanuts, chickens and cheap trinkets to sell to the African passengers aboard the ship. If the boat upsets as it is leaving the ship, it isn't too serious, for the men are all expert swimmers and their pirogues are usually almost empty. But if the boat overturns when it is loaded with produce, it represents a great loss to the owner. This afternoon I saw two boats capsize, spilling all of their contents into the water.

"Most of the cargo on our boat is from America - automobiles, tractors, and earth moving machinery which will be used in the building of roads in The Congo. On the return trip, the cargo will consist of palm oil, palm kernels, African oak which is used in the manufacture of television cabinets and furniture, and gold bars and bags of gold dust - much of which is destined for the USA.

"There are many aspects to travel in Africa that are most unpleasant—the dust and the heat and the insects to mention a few. But a trip up the Congo is a happy and wonderful adventure—providing the weather is in your favor as it happens to be this week."

The Palm Trees of Brabanta

Before proceeding into a description of my fourth African trip after my Congo River journey, I decided to make some changes in my plans.

When my boat landed at Brabanta, I was met by a Mr. Ungless, one of the supervisors of the plantation. He had been assigned to be my host during my visit. Mr. Ungless was an English gentleman who extended to me every courtesy. We traveled out to the plantation in his pickup truck and spent several hours watching the men at work.

One sight I shall never forget is that of a tree climber crawling to the top of a palm tree that was about a hundred feet in height—like the water towers in our Iowa towns. He is suspended in midair by a crude belt made from a palm leaf that goes around his body and the tree. With his bare feet planted firmly on the trunk, he holds himself at arm's length from the tree while the belt presses firmly against the small of his back. Now he reaches in his trouser belt and grasps his machete. He is ready to begin the job of cutting loose the cluster of palm fruit from the top of the tree.

In this precarious position, leaning backwards and suspended high above the ground, he swings his knife to cut loose the palm fruit. Suddenly a poisonous snake pokes out his head. It doesn't take the climber long to act. With one swift blow of his machete he cuts off the snake's head. Then he calmly goes on with his work. That brief incident gave me some idea of the danger involved in gathering palm fruit from which palm oil is obtained.

Those homemade belts gave me an uncomfortable feeling in the pit of my stomach. The vine which encircles the tree is less than an inch in thickness, and the back part of the belt, against which the climber throws the whole weight of his body, is the center rib of a palm leaf. Even the most skilled of the climbers sometimes misjudges his blow and strikes the belt with his razor sharp machete. The knife can easily sever the belt, plunging the climber into a backward somersault and a hundred feet to his death. Mr. Ungless informed me that this was the tragic experience of a climber just a couple of days before.

I asked Mr. Ungless about stories I had heard of the danger from poisonous tree climbing snakes.

"Those climbers must always be on the watch for them," he said. "The greatest danger is the horned viper. The bite of that viper is fatal ninety times out of a hundred.

And there doesn't seem to be a serum available that will give protection. One of the men was bitten by a horned viper just last week but the bite wasn't fatal. He lived to tell the story."

I looked at him incredulously.

"I thought you just said that the bite of a horned viper practically always results in death," I remarked.

"This man was lucky. The reason he survived the bite was that the snake had struck at the man's ankle and missed. It hit the tree instead and most of the venom went into the tree. Then he struck again and hit the man in the ankle, but most of the poison went into the tree. The man

TRUE TALES To Live By

Native climber scaling a palm tree.

was rushed to the hospital and he nearly died, but there wasn't quite enough poison to kill him."

In all of my African travels, I have had few other experiences that have given me such a feeling of admiration for the African as witnessing those two unforgettable events at the Brabanta Plantation.

Who among us would be willing to earn our daily bread climbing palm trees that tower to a height of a hundred feet? How many of us would be willing to toil and sweat day after day in a forest and jungle infested by poisonous snakes?

In our imagination, we see some of these men at the plantation lying in a hospital, or even their homes, with broken backs—some of them paralyzed for life because of falls from the palm trees. We think of the wives and their children who are saddened by these tragedies.

Some of us may say, "These occurrences are unfortunate, but why should these people who live thousands of miles across the sea be any concern of mine?

We must not forget that these tree climbers of The Congo are the men who gather for us the palm oil that is used in the making of our steel—the steel which goes into our automobiles, our airplanes and our farm machinery.

SKIP WESTPHAL

There are almost countless uses for steel, and the man who climbs the palm trees in the Congo plays a very important part in its manufacture. This just makes us realize that the health and welfare of the people of the Congo should be very much our concern, for their courage is woven into the fabric of our modern way of life.

The Fabulous Gold Mines of Johannesburg

On leaving the Palm Oil Plantation of Brabanta I traveled eastward to the gold mines in the vicinity of Johannesburg. What an inspiring experience it was!

There is gold dust under your feet here in South Africa's fabulous gold mining capital of the world. You know the gold is there as you walk the city streets or stroll along the country lanes. But most of it is down, way down, thousands of feet under the surface of the earth. The ground around Johannesburg is honeycombed with many miles of tunnels reaching out after the precious yellow gold. Most of the mines are connected for ventilation purposes and if you could walk in a straight line, you could follow these underground tunnels for over *one hundred miles* before coming to the surface!

I went down into a mine one day with Charles Barkley, an official of the Chamber of Mines in Johannesburg. We stepped into a small cage supported by a single cable, then down we went, straight down at a speed of thirty miles an hour, to a depth of over four thousand feet.

I didn't think about the danger at the moment, but later I heard that twelve miners had been killed in a fall when the cable on the elevator broke, plunging them several thousand feet to the bottom of the mine.

Stepping off the elevator we boarded a train which took us a distance of over a mile and a half. That was an interesting experience—traveling by train, four thousand feet below the surface of the earth. Then we proceeded on

145

foot for another half mile along a narrow dark tunnel, at the far end of which miners were at work drilling into the rock to prepare for blasting.

The noise of the jackhammers is deafening and the water dripping from the ceiling often spatters the miner with mud from head to foot. In spite of every precaution, his life is in constant danger from falling rock.

After the dynamite has been packed into the holes bored by the drills, the fuses are attached and the mine crew is alerted for the blast. All the explosions in the mine are set off at a given time each day; then the mine is deserted for several hours because of the danger of gas poisoning caused by the dynamite blast.

The average man would be completely exhausted after a few hours of such strenuous work, yet the African toils all day in the dampness and the mud. When he comes to the surface at the end of the days work, he still can sing. One is moved with a deep feeling of admiration for those weary, mud spattered miners who can come out of the elevator from that hot damp hole with a song on their lips. I heard some of them singing as they emerged from the elevator. It takes not only a strong body but a stout heart to show that kind of a spirit. I was doing no work, yet the coveralls I was wearing were wet with sweat.

That's where our wedding rings, our necklaces and our gold bracelets come from—down in the bowels of the earth where men are risking life and limb to get the precious yellow gold. Every few days in Johannesburg the newspapers carry a story about miners who have been killed, falling down a shaft or crushed by a cave-in.

As we emerged from the mine in the elevator we could see about us evidence of the tremendous amount of work expended to open the tunnels to get at the gold. The area around the reduction plant was surrounded with huge mountains of clay, sand and gravel which had been removed from the mines. The entire city of Johannesburg is surrounded by hundreds of these slime and gravel dumps, some of them built into pyramids which are over a mile square and a hundred feet tall. There are fifty mines operating in the Johannesburg area. Each one is surrounded by these mountains of dirt from which the gold has been removed.

Mr. Barkley informed me that it takes a ton of ore to make one ounce of gold. We passed by a pyramid of ore, possibly ten feet in height. At the very top was placed a thin rod, and at the end of the rod was a tiny piece of gold about the size of a kernel of corn. That represents the amount of ore that must be removed to obtain a small bit of gold.

It has often occurred to me that parents, as well as school teachers, can be compared to miners digging for gold. So much effort has to be spent which may appear to bring no results. How many times a mother has prayed, year after year for a wayward child, until her prayers are finally answered.

How often do adults feel that their words of advice "go in one ear and out the other?" Yet their effort may be compared to the task of digging for the gold. One day their efforts will hopefully appear in the form of fine citizens, Christian men and women who will be a credit to their parents and to the teachers who have labored with them.

Whenever we tend to become discouraged with the task of raising our children, we might do well to picture in our minds the gold miners of South Africa, blasting out a ton of rock to get one ounce of precious yellow gold. It takes work and sweat and tears, but it is well worth it in the end.

Acres of Diamonds

It was in the spring of 1867 that a little boy was playing in the gravel on the bank of the Orange River near Cape Town, South Africa. The pebbles of quartz, agate and jasper fascinated him. Every day he came down to the riverside to gather the pretty stones.

TRUE TALES To Live By

Suddenly he spied a pebble of unusual beauty. It had a sparkle such as he had never seen before. Clutching it in his hands, little Erasmus Jacobs ran to his mother to show her what he had found.

Mrs. Jacobs wasn't particularly interested in it and tossed the stone into her workbasket with some of the other pebbles that the boy had brought to her from the riverbank.

One day a neighbor, Schalk van Niekerk, stopped by for a visit and noticed the boy, his two sisters and two brothers playing a game know as *five stones*. They were using ordinary stones, but one of them caught the eye of Mr. van Niekerk, and he offered to buy it. Mrs. Jacobs scoffed at the idea that the stone had any value and although she was a poor farmer's wife, she refused to accept any money for it.

Van Niekerk turned the stone over to an acquaintance, a peddler by the name of O'Reilly, who took it to an assayer. The sparkling stone proved to be a diamond and was eventually sold for five hundred pounds, the equivalent of eight hundred dollars in our money today.

That was the beginning of the fabulous diamond industry in South Africa. However, it took a couple of years after the boy found the diamond on the riverbank before any diamonds of real value were found. In fact, van Niekerk began to wonder if that first stone which had created such a sensation had been carried in the gizzard of an ostrich from some far distant place.

Then one day the electrifying news spread throughout the countryside that a Griqua shepherd boy had found a diamond much larger than the one which had been picked up by Erasmus Jacobs. Van Niekerk searched out the boy and was so impressed by the size and beauty of the stone that he bought it for five hundred sheep, ten oxen and a horse. To the shepherd boy that was a fabulous price, but he had no idea that his discovery, an 83.5 carat diamond later named The Star of South Africa, would one day bring a price of twenty-five thousand pounds (forty thousand dollars).

Within a few months after the discovery of The Star of Africa, more diamonds were found in the area of what was known as Klip Drift, and within two years, over ten thousand adventurers from all over the world were pouring into the mining camp of Kimberly. A poor farm boy, a peddler and a shepherd had unwittingly begun one of the most exciting chapters in the history of South Africa. Thousands of people were destined to make fortunes from South Africa's diamonds, but the boy who found the first stone never made a penny from it. Many years later, as an old man, he complained bitterly that he had not received even a shilling from his diamond discovery.

The amazing part of the diamond discovery was that these precious stones had been lying on the ground in plain sight for years. Children had played with them; ostriches had swallowed them; cattle and sheep had trampled them into the mud. No one seemed to know they existed and were worth a fortune until that day when the poor farmer's boy picked up the precious stone from the gravel on the riverbank. There were acres of diamonds under the feet of these South African farmers, but they were unaware of their value.

What a story I had to tell on the radio program I was planning about the discovery of diamonds in Africa!

An old proverb says, "Every man has a goose that lays golden eggs if he only knew it." That truth applied to many of the landowners in South Africa.

Not all of the diamond diggers found the treasure they were looking for. One prospector would strike it rich in a few hours while another, working an adjoining claim just a few feet away, would struggle for months without finding enough diamonds to pay his grocery bill.

Not all of the diamonds were dug from far below the surface of the earth. Some were found right under the prospector's feet. One day a Southwest African hunter killed an ostrich. Upon opening the bird, he was amazed to find a beautiful diamond in its gizzard. He tried to keep his exciting discovery a secret but somehow the news got out

TRUE TALES To Live By

and it touched off a wild rush to go prospecting for diamonds in ostrich gizzards.

Within a short time, adventurers from all over Africa were swarming into the area to hunt for ostriches. Soon hundreds of diamonds were found in ostrich gizzards until the big birds became very scarce.

There is the story of an American schoolteacher who had gone to Africa for her summer vacation. She had spent the day wandering along the beach and on returning to her hotel was removing her shoes to empty out the sand. As she turned over her shoe, a diamond fell to the floor. The lady was overjoyed with her discovery until she found that smuggling an uncut diamond from the country could result in a heavy fine and even imprisonment. She decided not to keep the diamond!

To get more of the diamond story, I contacted a gentleman who had just what I wanted. He was Major C. E. Young, mining official in charge of the diamond prospecting area northwest of Kimberly. He was scheduled to make an inspection trip the following day, and he invited me to accompany him.

A half-hour drive and we came to a sign marked "To the Diggings." After several miles over a very bumpy road we arrived at the banks of a small stream and a cluster of prospectors' shacks.

Soon we came to an area where a group of about fifty men were at work. Some of the men were down in the bottom of holes about ten feet deep, digging with picks and shovels. The man who had staked out the claim shook the gravel from a pan onto a small table. Slowly and painstakingly he scanned every bit of the ore which might contain a sparkling diamond that might make him rich the rest of his life.

"You may wonder why these fellows are willing to work for months with little to show for their efforts," remarked Major Young. "Just a few rods from here, a diamond was recently found worth $51,548. Another such valuable diamond may not be found for weeks or months; yet some lucky prospector may find one at any moment."

We walked over to a bewhiskered prospector who was carefully scanning a pile of gravel on a small table. "This man," said Major Young, "is Fred Jacobus Van Zyl. He's about seventy years old and has been searching for diamonds for over fifty years."

"What is the most valuable diamond you have ever found," I asked the old prospector.

"I picked up a stone once worth about seven thousand dollars," he replied, but my debts totaled about eight thousand dollars, so that didn't leave me anything to celebrate about."

"How much do you have to show for your fifty years of diamond digging?" Major Young asked.

"I have nothing to show for it," the old gentleman replied with a chuckle. "All of the diamonds I have ever found went into wages for my help, grocery bills and living expenses. The debts begin to pile up on you; then you find a few stones to pay off your debts and you're ready to start over again."

"But I have no regrets," he added. "Perhaps one day I'll find a big one. Anyway, it's a fascinating business and once it gets hold of you, there's nothing much you can do about it."

Here was a man who had spent his entire lifetime searching for *the pot of gold at the end of the rainbow*, but had failed to find it. One might say his whole life had been a failure. Yet, had he actually failed? Fred Van Zyl might have been a bitter disillusioned old man. Some of the miners had committed suicide because of their failures. But after all these years of failure he had not lost his sense of humor. He was still able to chuckle at the thought that he had nothing to show for a lifetime of hard work. That in itself is an accomplishment of which a man had reason to be proud. He has made many friends at the diggings and given jobs to many Africans who were desperately in need of food for their hungry children.

TRUE TALES To Live By

As I visited with this old prospector, I recalled my friendship with the poet Edwin Markham. This poet, with his twinkling eyes and bushy beard, bore a close resemblance to Fred Van Zyl.

Said Mr. Markham to me one day, "I look upon the disappointments of life as mere flyspecks on the map! Therefore I never lose courage but keep the high heart singing as I press on."

The old poet expressed his optimistic philosophy in the lines of one of his many poems.

I am done with the years that were, I am quits,
They are mines worked out; I delved in their pits.
I have saved their grain of gold.
Now I turn to the future for wine and bread.
I have bidden the past adieu,
I laugh and lift hands to the years ahead.
Come on: I am ready for you.

After leaving the prospecting area near Kimberly, I traveled into the bush country of the Congo to visit Bakwanga, the largest industrial diamond mine in the world. That's where the diamonds are obtained not for jewels, but for grinding tools in modern industry. My journey to Bakwanga took several days by riverboat, then continued on a very slow and dirty train to Luluabourg and by plane over jungle country to Bakwanga.

The European section of the city of Bakwanga is quite modern with many beautiful homes, movie theatres, swimming pools and even air conditioned supermarkets. The homes that the company had built for its workers were neat, attractive cottages. These beautiful surroundings are in sharp contrast to the mud huts from which most of the workers came.

I had written the company headquarters several weeks previously concerning my plans to visit the mines, so when I reported to the main office I was met by Fernand van Wynsberghe in the research department. He was very accommodating and helped me collect material for the radio program I had taped during my visit.

SKIP WESTPHAL

The operation at Bakwanga consists of *open pit* mining. In some areas the diamonds can be found within a foot of the surface. Elsewhere, it may be necessary to dig down sixty feet or more to the area that is rich in diamonds. Here at the mines, equipment valued at millions of dollars of equipment is employed. There are fifteen bulldozers and huge drag lines, twelve caterpillar tractors and sixty-five twenty-ton trucks hauling the gravel.

It is not an easy matter to secure permission to the sorting room. Mr. Van Wynsberghe escorted me through the area.

To remove the diamonds, the gravel is run through vibrating grease tables that the other minerals pass over. Here fifteen skilled African workers handpick the gravel that contains the diamonds. Each man has his head shaved and is kept under close supervision.

Many stories are told about the attempts by native miners to smuggle out diamonds. When one of the men was about to be discharged, his strange conduct aroused the suspicion of the examiner. The man was given a laxative and it was found that he had swallowed twenty-one diamonds worth several thousand dollars.

One man at work in the sorting room appeared to be developing symptoms of tetanus. The doctor examined him and found that the man had made an incision under his shin bone in which he had hidden a rag full of diamonds.

The diamond has the magic power which takes the African out of his grass hut, gives him a comfortable home in which to live, and provides his children with an education.

So we are led to the conclusion that the diamond blesses the man who digs it from the earth and it enriches the life of every man and woman and child in the civilized world.

TRUE TALES To Live By

Cobalt, a Nuisance Metal?

The fourth stop in my tour of Africa sponsored by the Ford Foundation was the Kolwezi cobalt mines in the southern Congo.

It was about two months after my visit to the pharmaceutical plant in Chicago that I stood on the rim of one of the biggest man-made holes I had ever seen—the Kolwezi cobalt mines. This hole is about a half-mile wide, three-and-a-half miles long and four hundred fifty feet deep. Most of the world's supply of cobalt comes from this huge hole. Cobalt is almost as valuable as gold and has many uses, so I was amazed when I was told by mining officials that it was once considered to be a *nuisance metal*.

That observation reminded me of a quotation by Lord Pahnerston: "Dirt is not dirt, but something in the wrong place." Not only with cobalt, but many areas of life, that which was once considered useless waste, is now recognized as having great value. One example of this is the way in which the city of Chicago is now using its sanitation wastes to fertilize crops of corn, soybeans and alfalfa. The garbage that was once burned and considered an expensive nuisance, is now raising bountiful crops of grain. Smelly, sanitation sludge is now being turned into *liquid gold*, and the clouds of smoke from garbage dumps no longer pollute the air. The United States has been slow in adopting this happy solution to the garbage disposal problem. The use of sludge in farming operations has long been practiced in Europe, Israel and Australia.

Recently the newspapers carried accounts of a new method that has been developed to make use of the smoke from industrial plants. It has been discovered that the black clouds of smoke that belch from factory chimneys can be turned into bricks. These bricks are cheaper, lighter and more durable than bricks made from clay.

The accounts of the wealth that is to be found in garbage and factory smoke can be repeated in the history of the discovery of the precious metal cobalt. Once it was thrown into the dump heap along with the dirt and useless rocks. The miners of the Congo had no idea that they were casting away a substance which in many respects was more precious than gold. Today it has scores of uses. It is widely used in the treatment of cancer. I have seen a lead ball in a cancer clinic that contains twelve silvery discs, each about the size of a penny. Those discs are radio activated cobalt worth over twenty thousand dollars.

Cobalt is used in the alloy alnico, to make powerful magnets in radios and television equipment. Another alloy, elgiloy, which is composed of cobalt, chromium and nickel, is used in making watch springs. Since the metal cobalt retains its hardness at temperatures of one thousand degrees centigrade, it is employed in the construction of jet propelled airplanes and guided missiles. This metal is also used in feed for hogs, sheep and cattle, and is an important ingredient in medicines for both livestock and human beings. At one time miners discarded it as being absolutely useless!

A look at the cobalt mines reminds us not to overlook what may appear to be waste in life, like the miners who once discarded the valuable cobalt.

INTERESTING PEOPLE WHO HAVE CROSSED MY PATHWAY

SKIP WESTPHAL

Don't Saw Off that Leg

The most rewarding aspect of my travels in some forty countries, has been meeting the interesting people who have crossed my path. One of them was a president of the United States, Dwight Eisenhower.

I met him in Ames, Iowa, when he was campaigning for president. The slogan which swept over the country at that time was, "I Like Ike." I still have the button I wore with those three words. He was probably one of the most popular, and best loved of all our presidents.

My brother Earl and I were among the delegates at the Iowa State Convention that helped to nominate him. After my meeting with Ike, I was so impressed by his friendly manner, I decided to do some research on his life. I discovered the following story about one of his boyhood experiences.

In a small Midwestern town about seventy-five years ago, a boy fell while running home from school and hurt his knee. The leg swelled so alarmingly that the doctor insisted it must be amputated. The boy kept repeating over and over, "Don't let anyone saw off that leg!"

The members of his family were devoted Christians who believed strongly in the power of prayer. For two days and two nights the parents, grandfather and brothers took turns kneeling by the boy's bedside praying for his recovery. The boys

"More things are wrought by prayer than this world dreams of."
Alfred Lord Tennyson

I HAVE BEEN DRIVEN MANY TIMES TO MY KNEES BY THE OVERWHELMING CONVICTION THAT I HAD NOWHERE ELSE TO GO
• • •
MY OWN WISDOM AND THAT OF ALL ABOUT ME SEEMED INSUFFICIENT

A. Lincoln

Trust in the Lord with all thine heart and lean not unto thine own understanding. In all thy ways acknowledge Him and He shall direct thy paths.
—Proverbs 3:5

TRUE TALES To Live By

took turns doing the chores and kneeling at the bedside with the family to pray that the leg would be healed.

On the second night the family was overjoyed to see that the swelling in the leg was going down. They called for the doctor and he was amazed to see that the leg was returning to normal.

Had that boy's leg been amputated it would have changed the history of our country. He would not have been admitted to West Point. He would not have served as supreme commander of the United States Armed Forces in Europe during World War II. He would not have become president of the United States. That boy was Dwight Eisenhower.

The Friendly Cobbler

Many years ago in Northampton, Massachusetts, a cobbler plied his trade. His customers enjoyed their friendly chats with James Lucey. He came from Old Ireland and was known for his Irish sense of humor. Little did his friends realize that the influence of this humble cobbler would one day extend beyond Massachusetts to every state in the land.

One of Lucey's friends was a student who attended a college in Northampton. He often relaxed from his studies to visit with his cobbler friend.

The student was undecided as to the career he would pursue upon his graduation from college. He was not interested in politics but at James Lucey's urging he finally decided to give it a try.

The advice of James Lucey had a great deal of influence on that young man for, due to his persistence and faith in his ability, he won election to the state legislature, then became governor of Massachusetts and eventually vice president of the United States.

At the sudden death of President Harding, he became president of the United States. The oath of office was administered by his father, a Justice of the Peace, by the light of a kerosene lamp in his farm home in Plymouth, Vermont.

One day while serving as an English teacher in Manchester, New Hampshire, I visited James Lucey in his shoemaker's shop in Northampton. Hanging on the wall above his cobbler's bench was a framed letter that Mr. Lucey told me was written the day after the president was sworn in as president of the United States. It read as follows:

> "It's a good safe rule to sojourn in every place as if you meant to spend your life there, never omitting an opportunity of doing a kindness, speaking a true word, or making a friend."
> — John Ruskin

Be kindly affectioned one to another with brotherly love, in honor preferring one another.
—Romans 12:14

THE WHITE HOUSE
Washington, D.C.

My Dear Mr. Lucey:

If it had not been for you, I would not be here. I have long considered you to be my guide, philosopher and friend.

Sincerely,
Calvin Coolidge

Was This Man a Failure?

A friend of mine, Dr. Ashton McCrary of the McCrary-Rost Clinic in Lake City, Iowa, took pleasure in passing on to me true stories which he thought I could use in my weekly newspaper column. I'm very grateful to him for one of the most unusual stories he shared with me. It was about a man known as John Pierpont.

On graduating from college, he decided that his calling was that of a teacher. He started out in that profession with a great deal of enthusiasm. It wasn't long, however, before he was faced with disturbing situations that he hadn't anticipated. Whether it was discipline problems with his students or lack of cooperation from the parents, we do not know but he soon came to the conclusion that teaching school was not for him.

For years he had been attracted to the life of a lawyer. It meant spending more years in college to pass the bar exam, but he decided to give it a try.

The time came when he set up his law office and started out on a new career. But as with his experience as a teacher, he soon became disillusioned with the law profession. He might have continued in a work that he intensely disliked had not some friends encouraged him to enter the Christian ministry.

Again that meant more college training, this time in a Christian seminary. When he completed his studies, he was pleased to receive a call from a church in Washington, D.C.

At last, after failures in teaching and in the practice of law, he had found his niche. The members of his congregation welcomed him warmly. He regretted that he hadn't entered the ministry when he first graduated from college. What a joy it was to be the admired and loved shepherd of his flock in that church.

As had happened before, there came a road block in his career. It was at the time of the Civil War and Rev. Pierpont preached with his whole heart against slavery. There were several members of his congregation who had lived in the South and bitterly resented his preaching against the practice of slavery. In spite of his popularity with the vast majority of the congregation, he was forced to resign. I've been told that this happens in many churches. A few members can often, with falsehoods and misrepresentations, force a pastor's resignation.

I know of one pastor who had a heart attack after his forced resignation and died within a short time. Some of his loyal supporters said, "He died of a broken heart."

That didn't happen to John Pierpont but he spent his last days disappointed at his failure. He finally secured a poorly paid federal job in an office in Washington, D.C.

He was not aware that, unknown to himself, he was a tremendous success. One Christmas he wrote a song for his family. It was not well known at first, but after his death, that song warmed the hearts of millions upon millions of children and adults all over the world. The song: "Jingle Bells."

John Wayne Inspired a Song

One would not expect that attendance at a state fair in Des Moines, Iowa, would be a very unusual experience, but one year it was for me.

While at the fair grounds, I attended a service at a little church where Stuart Hamblin, a well-known songwriter, was the speaker. After the service, I had the pleasure of visiting with him. I was fascinated by his story of how his song, "It Is No Secret," was written.

Hamblin told of how he had a reputation in Hollywood of being a hopeless alcoholic. One evening he attended a Billy Graham evangelistic rally. He decided to become a Christian and *went on the wagon*. The word went around among his friends that Stuart Hamblin had not taken another drink since the Billy Graham rally.

One evening John Wayne, a friend of Hamblin, called at his home for a visit. Wayne was puzzled about how his friend had been able to break the drinking habit after several years of being an alcoholic.

Said Hamblin, "It is no secret what God can do."

As John Wayne was about to leave the Hamblin home that night, he stopped at the door, put his hand on his

TRUE TALES To Live By

friend's shoulder and with a smile made this suggestion, "Stuart, why don't you write a song titled, *It Is No Secret, What God Can Do.*"

After John Wayne left, Hamblin sat down at the piano. As his fingers ran over the keys, he began to think about his friend's suggestion. Would those eight words be the inspiration for a song?

He remembers that the clock struck twelve as the words and the music began to form in his mind. Without any effort, the music flowed from his fingers onto the keys of the piano.

When he had the feeling that he had completed the song, he looked up at the clock. The hands stood at twelve fifteen. He was amazed to realize that in fifteen minutes he had written the words and the music to a beautiful song that would be a blessing and an inspiration to many.

The John Wayne inspired song:

> It is no secret, what God can do.
> What He's done for others,
> He'll do for you.
> With arms wide open,
> He'll pardon you.
> It is no secret,
> what God can do.

Grandmother to over 100 Thousand Orphans

Harry Holt, a West Coast lumberman, suffered a heart attack one day while felling trees on an Oregon mountainside. He was carried by his fellow workers to his home in Creswell.

Bed-ridden for several weeks, he heard over the radio heart-breaking stories of orphaned children who were abandoned as a result of the war in Korea. Many were sleeping under bridges or in cardboard boxes and were eating out of garbage cans. Dedicated *born again* Christians, he and his wife Bertha prayed about what they could do to help those unfortunate children. Although they had six of their own, they finally decided to adopt eight of those abandoned orphans.

Harry made a trip to Korea to investigate the situation. On his flight to Korea he was not quite sure that God had called him to help arrange for the adoption of Korean children. He checked in at a hotel in Tokyo on his way.

As he retired to his room for the night, he wrote a letter to his wife. Following is an excerpt from that letter indicating that he was beginning to question whether his courage was beginning to fail him about this Korean orphan project.

"As these thoughts filled my mind I became very discouraged and I finally slipped out of bed and knelt down and poured my distress out to the Lord. That didn't seem to help very much and I finally said, 'Lord, my faith is very small this morning. Will You show me from Your Word whether I'm doing this myself or whether You are with me?' Then I shook my Bible open and put my thumb on part of the page and turned on the light. Out of all the wonderful Word of God, I had my thumb pointing to these words, in Isaiah 43:5-7: 'Fear not for I am with thee.' This so affected me that I was unable to finish reading the context and could only thank God for the direct answer to prayer. Later on, when I read the Scripture again and read the context, I could hardly believe my eyes. Listen to it: 'I will bring thy seed from the east, and gather thee from the west; I will say to the north, Give up; and to the south, Keep not back: bring my sons from far, and my daughters from the ends of the earth; even every one that is called by my name: for I have created him for my glory, I have formed him; yea, I have made him.'"

"I realize, of course, that this had been written as a prophecy about the regathering of Israel in the end times, but the Word of God is quick and powerful, or as the Revised Version puts it, living and active, and I felt that this was for me. It even gave me a wonderful thought—perhaps

TRUE TALES To Live By

This little girl was adopted by an American couple. Had it not been for the Holt orphanage and her adoptive parents, she would have been an outcast.

God might use me to save even more of His little ones than the eight that we hope to bring back.

"I just had to get down and weep before the Lord. Love, Daddy."

Shortly after his arrival in Korea Harry Holt was joined by his wife and their children. During the bitter cold winter months, the parents and their fourteen children lived in a tent, twenty-six feet by twenty feet, while plans were being made to build an orphanage.

Harry had made over a million dollars in his lumber business, and he spent practically all of it in building the home for abandoned children. From all over Korea, poverty stricken mothers brought their babies to the orphanage. A tiny baby, wrapped in a blanket, was found one morning in a snow bank near the orphanage entrance. The mother, no doubt feared that there might not be room for the baby, so she probably watched from a distance until a nurse picked up the baby and carried it into the warm shelter.

Then there is the story of a, boy who on rainy nights slept under railroad cars for shelter. One night, he didn't realize that one foot was over the rail. While the boy was sleeping, the train moved ahead and crushed the boy's foot. Almost fainting from the shock of the injury, he managed to wrap his leg with a rag to stop the bleeding. He found a stick for a cane and, although it seemed like a miracle, he hobbled about for two days with that injured leg, sleeping in back alleys and picking up any scraps of food he could find. He finally collapsed from the pain of the wound and the gangrene in the wounded leg.

Finally, an American soldier found the boy and carried him to a hospital the Holts had built. There the boy was treated for his injury and soon recovered. He was later adopted by a family in the United States.

The story of how the Holts had been successful in adopting those eight Korean orphans spread to the United States. Letters from parents who longed to have children started to pour in and the Holt Adoption Program was launched.

Their deep Christian faith inspired in their hearts a love for children who were in need. Had it not been for their love for the Lord, this amazing story of the Holt Adoption Program would never have been written.

Harry Holt's stamina and persistence is shown by the following incident.

After two serious heart attacks, he was told by his doctor that he never would be able to make another trip across the Pacific. He proved the doctor wrong by making seventy-seven flights to Korea to organize and promote the Holt Adoption Program.

Several years ago, the work of the adoption program proved to be such a strain on Harry Holt that he died of a heart attack. His wife, Bertha, carried on the work and the Korean Government honored her by giving her the title of "Korean Mother of the Year."

My wife, Marion, and I made a trip to Korea with fifty-two American couples who had made arrangements to adopt Korean orphans. One couple had six children of their own and they planned to adopt six more so that each of them would be responsible for a child. Our plane, The Flying Tiger, returned to the States with eighty children aboard.

Marion and I had adopted three-year-old Kimberly. We shall always remember the trip home with her. As the plane left Seoul, Marion was holding Kimberly on her lap. The seat beside her remained empty. All of the way across the Pacific, that little girl insisted on sitting on Marion's lap. She evidently felt secure with her new mother and feared she might lose her as she had lost her native mother.

Since almost all of her contacts in the orphanage were with women, Kimberly ignored me until we reached Anchorage, Alaska. At the airport waiting room she reluctantly allowed me to hold her as we stroked the back of a huge stuffed polar bear. Then I was rewarded by her first smile and we were friends from then on.

The Des Moines, Iowa, Register, reporting on this unusual flight from Korea, ran a headline on a story I wrote on our return. The headline read, "From Korea They Brought Back a Planeload of Happiness."

Several months after our arrival back home we decided that Kimberly needed a sister. We arranged for the adoption of another three-year-old girl named Sunia, from Korea. She arrived at Chicago by plane. What a happy meeting with our little Sunia.

Words cannot express how these two Korean girls have blessed our home through the years.

Kimberly at the present time is working on assembling custom computer programs for hospitals.

Sunia has been working on a medical surgical floor, but is transferring to the business office where she will be auditing records to verify charges, insurance settlements, etc.

SKIP WESTPHAL

Okotambulu and the Elephant

One evening I attended a young people's meeting at the Methodist Church in Manson, Iowa. The speaker at that meeting was Burleigh Law, a missionary on leave after several years in the Belgian Congo.

Burleigh told the amazing story about a friend of his, a native African named Okotambulu, who was run through by the tusk of an angry elephant...and lived. To Burleigh's knowledge, no one has ever been run through by the tusk of an elephant and survived.

The most thrilling part of the story was that while in a mission hospital, the doctor and nurses witnessed to Okotambulu of their faith and he became a dedicated Christian. He was so excited about his newfound faith, that on his release from the hospital he built seven new churches in jungle country.

I was so impressed by this inspiring story that I resolved I would make a trip to Africa and meet Okotambulu.

A bachelor at that time, I was footloose and fancy free. I had a small farm but no livestock, so in the winter months I was free to travel. My mother, who kept house for me, was amazed when I came home from that meeting and told her I was going to make a trip to Africa. She moved over to my sister's who lived on a nearby farm, and I took off.

In a few days, I booked passage on an ocean liner headed for Leopoldville, which at that time was the capital of the Belgian Congo. Traveling by bus and by air, I soon

TRUE TALES To Live By

arrived at the Methodist Mission at Wembo Nyama. I was given a warm welcome by Dr. Hughlett at the mission hospital. He immediately sent a runner to a nearby village where Okotambulu lived and requested that he come to the mission to meet a visitor from America who wished to see him.

I shall never forget the interesting meeting I had with Okotambulu. He told me about his frightening experience when attacked by the elephant. He spoke in broken English with Dr. Hughlett acting as his interpreter.

I decided that it would be more realistic and more exciting to tell his story in a poem. So here follows the exciting experience which Okotambulu told to me that day as we stood beneath a tree on the grounds of this Wembo Nyama Mission.

Okotambulu and the Elephant

An African, Okotambulu, was traveling in jungle country one day
When he heard the trumpet of an elephant not far away.
He started to climb a tree
There from danger he would be free.

Before he could reach the nearest limb
The angry elephant was upon him.
Into his back with a mighty thrust
She lifted him in the air with her powerful tusk.

As he fell at her feet crying out in pain
The elephant left him for her little one
Who was calling again and again.

Okotambulu from loss of blood would have died
Had not some hunters passing by at his side.
To a nearby hospital they carried the wounded man
They feared there was no hope, try as doctors can.
But a miracle happened.
After days of no hope
The bleeding stopped and the fever broke.

One day he said to his nurse, "You work so hard and so long
Yet you always are happy and always have a song."

The nurse replied, "The reason there's a song in our hearts
Is that day after day we have Jesus in our hearts."

Okotambulu was so impressed by the nurses' loving care
That he decided to become a Christian, it was an answer
 to prayer.
Soon after he found the Lord, Okotambulu became well
He was eager to get home the good news to tell.

When he returned to Kikugu, the village that he loved
His friends were sure he was from Heaven above.
How could a man be run through by an elephant's tusk,
And he live to tell it, that could not be.

When he showed them the big scar on his chest
They decided that it really was not just a jest.
The Chief called for the drummer "Send out the word
Okotambulu is alive! His message should be heard."

The chiefs of those jungle villages, seven in all,
Eagerly asked Okotambulu to answer their call.
He told so eagerly about the Saviour he knew
That most of the people wanted to know him, too.

They asked that he visit them again and again.
He built not one, but seven churches many souls to win.

Added note: Isn't it wonderful how God was able to use the attack of an angry elephant to reach the hearts of hundreds of his people.

The Lost Wedding Ring

The interesting people who have crossed my pathway are sometimes famous like Dwight Eisenhower or Albert Schweitzer. Many of the folks I have met are not famous but they have an unusual story to tell.

Edna Holtan, a homemaker from Thor, Iowa, was—with her husband—a member of a tour group Marion and I hosted to the Scandinavian countries.

On our return from the trip, we were entertained in their home for an evening meal. During our conversation, Edna told us an amazing story about her wedding ring.

TRUE TALES To Live By

She told how she was busy one day mixing dough for a batch of bread. She had taken off her wedding ring and placed it on a corner of the mixing board. After she had placed the dough in the oven, she gathered up the scraps and threw them over the fence to the chickens.

On returning to the kitchen, she looked for her ring but it was nowhere to be found. Her family searched for it several days without success. Her prayers for the recovery of the ring seemed to be of no avail.

Years passed, and one night a terrific windstorm swept through the area, destroying some of the choice apple trees in the family orchard. The Holtans were saddened by the devastation that was caused by the storm.

The next morning Edna's husband was hard at work clearing out the broken limbs and trees when he spotted something glistening on the end of one of the branches. He climbed the tree and found, to his amazement, that it was his wife's lost wedding ring! Near the ring was a shattered bird nest.

It was Edna's birthday and the family decided to share the wonderful surprise with her at the birthday dinner that evening. The ring was hidden in a piece of apple pie. When the time came for dessert and Edna's fork struck that precious wedding ring, one can imagine her surprise. What a celebration at that birthday dinner!

An Inspiring Poster in a Restroom

One day my wife and I were passing through Liberal, Kansas. We stopped for lunch in a restaurant and were amazed to see on the wall of the restroom a poster with a beautiful picture of a cross with this inspiring spiritual message: "The nails did not hold Jesus to the cross. It was His love for you and me."

We met the owner of the restaurant and learned that she had once been an alcoholic and a drug addict. She described how she would put her two children to bed and then go out and walk the streets. She added, "I had hit rock bottom and the only way to look was up—to my Heavenly Father."

She concluded her testimony with the statement, "I am now married to an ex-convict who became a Christian while reading the Bible from cover to cover in a prison cell."

The lady now has a family, several children, and they are all very active in a church in their community.

On leaving the restaurant, this remarkable lady gave me a copy of the poster. When we returned to our home church, the Evangelical Free Church of Fort Dodge, Iowa, we showed the poster to our Christian friends, and they enthusiastically contributed twelve hundred dollars to having it reproduced for two months on an illuminated billboard beside one of the busy streets of the city.

From a wall of a Kansas restaurant restroom to the billboard in Fort Dodge, Iowa, the message shone forth a beacon light to an estimated ten thousand cars which passed that way each day.

Many stories could be told of how travelers who passed by the billboard were inspired. One passerby wrote a letter saying that, inspired by the billboard message, she had returned to her church after a long absence.

Sometimes an insignificant event proves to be of great importance. Suppose we would not have stopped for lunch at that particular restaurant. What an inspiring experience we would have missed!

TRUE TALES To Live By

Meeting with Joni Eareckson

Marion and I had the pleasure of going to a Congress on the Church and the Disabled that was held in Wheaton, Illinois. It was a most unusual experience. In attendance at the meetings were representatives from forty states and several foreign countries. Many were in wheelchairs; some were on crutches; a number were there with seeing-eye dogs.

This unusual get-together was the brainchild of Joni Eareckson Tada. Joni is known by millions around the world for her artistic accomplishments, in spite of the broken neck she suffered at age seventeen in a diving accident. She was paralyzed from the shoulders down. Joni has learned to draw with her mouth. She signs her drawings, "Joni, PTL." The letters mean "Praise the Lord."

Joni has appeared on numerous television programs. She was interviewed by Barbara Walters on the *Today Show* and is the author of several books which have been read by millions.

It was a rare privilege for Marion and I to meet this remarkable lady and to hear her give the keynote address at the conference. Her experience is certainly an excellent example of the quotation by the Persian poet, Nizami, which is the title of one of my books, "In the hour of adversity, be not without hope for crystal rain falls from black clouds."

In her address, Joni told how in the early days after her accident, when her arms were immovable, she was greatly distressed at being unable to scratch her nose when it itched. She became resigned to this discomfort when she realized that the Lord Jesus, as He hung on the cross, was also not able to scratch his nose. After years of physical therapy, Joni is now able to enjoy some movement in her arms, although she must still rely on her mouth for holding her pen and brush.

The theme of the conference was a challenge to the churches to assume more responsibility in ministering to the disabled. I could spend considerable time describing the interesting people we met at the conference. One of my most poignant experiences was the sight of a very pretty little girl, probably nine or ten years of age, eating with her toes. She took a cracker from her mother and held it between her toes when the refreshments were served.

The Amazing Story of Bob Wieland

Another speaker at the conference was Bob Wieland. Both his legs were blown off when he stepped on a mine in Vietnam. He was taken to the Army hospital by a helicopter and pronounced DOA—dead on arrival. However, although unconscious for five days, he recovered from his wounds.

In Vietnam he witnessed much suffering among the starving children. After his return to the states, his physical condition improved to such an extent that he was able to make an amazing journey, walking across America on his hands. The purpose of his trip was to raise funds for the starving children of the world. He succeeded in raising several hundred thousand dollars for this worthy cause by inviting people to contribute a certain amount for each step he took.

We first met Bob while he was walking across America. We invited him to enjoy a meal with us at a nearby restaurant. He told us how a small boy sitting on a curb, saw him coming down the road, and ran to meet him with seventeen cents to help feed hungry children. Bob described his tragic accident in these words.

"I was assigned one day to a patrol to conduct raids against the Viet Cong in the dense jungles north of Saigon. We didn't realize that we had walked into the open end of a *horseshoe* ambush. The enemy opened fire from three sides and my dead and wounded buddies fell all around me. As I saw a friend go down, I ran to him and suddenly everything went black. I had stepped on and detonated a hidden eighty-two millimeter mortal round. An explosive designed to blow up a tank ripped me in half. My legs were blown right off my body. Blood poured onto the ground as I lost consciousness.

"That's when my Heavenly Father began an astonishing series of miracles in my life. A chopper pilot deviated from his scheduled route and found me in the jungle. Twenty minutes later I was on the operating table. I was losing blood rapidly and my blood pressure went to almost zero. I wasn't breathing, so they performed a tracheotomy, cutting a hole in my throat to pump oxygen back into my lungs.

"It was necessary to replenish my entire blood supply. Later, doctors told me that if I had lain fifteen seconds longer in that Vietnam field, it would have been too late.

"I still get goose bumps just thinking about the grace of God which allowed me to live."

At first as he lay on his bed in the army hospital he found his crippling condition hard to accept. Before being drafted into the service, he had aspired to play professional baseball with the Phillies. He had been accepted and was negotiating the contract when Uncle Sam gave him the invitation to join the army. Now his dream of an athletic career was ended.

Bob soon began to realize, however, that even without legs, he still had a great deal for which to be thankful. He might have been killed in that blast, or—like many other Vietnam veterans—he could have been blinded or paralyzed for life in that tragic explosion. His fighting spirit and his deep faith in God helped him overcome his depression and resolve to make something of his life in spite of his handicap.

While serving in Vietnam, Bob had witnessed a great deal of suffering from hunger on the part of the Vietnamese people. He was particularly depressed at the sight of little children half starved and begging for food. He often wished that there was something he could do about it. But what could one man do in the face of such misery? Now as he lay in the hospital bed realizing that he was only *half a man*, it seemed utterly impossible that he could make even a dent on the problem of world hunger. Yet he continued to be haunted by the words of the Lord Jesus, "For I was an hungered and ye gave me no meat; I was thirsty and ye gave me no drink...as ye did it not to one of the least of these, ye did it not to me." Perhaps the Lord, he thought, will enable me to obey that admonition even in my crippled condition.

On returning to the States, he decided to use weight lifting to rehabilitate his broken body.

"I see the Walk for Hunger," he says, "as a significant tool in helping to end hunger. Vietnam was my first glimpse of the ravages of hunger, and I vowed then and there to someday do something to help people who have no hope. I saw little children with no shoes risk their lives by running into burning garbage dumps to get a little rotten food."

On September 8, 1982, Bob began his Walk for Hunger at Knott's Berry Farm in Buena Park, California. By averaging five miles a day, he believed he could reach the steps of the White House in early 1984.

Bob measured his trip across the continent in terms of *steps*, which for him was a forward thrust by his arms that covered three feet. Each step was to be sponsored and he hoped to raise more than twenty million dollars for the hungry.

It took Bob three months to reach the California-Arizona border. Here he learned that through contributions of friends and the cooperation of an overseas airline, he would be offered the opportunity to make a ten-day trip west to visit orphanages, hospitals and refugee camps in Hong Kong, Bangkok, Dacca and other cities in the Far East. In Calcutta, he toured Mother Teresa's Home for the Destitute and Dying.

I was in Phoenix when Bob talked to the press at the conclusion of his tour. During this press conference, he gave a dramatic report of what he saw on the tour.

TRUE TALES To Live By

"I saw visually the horrible things which you can't even imagine," he said. "I spent most of the trip with my mouth open, because I couldn't believe what I was seeing was real. I saw eleven-month-old children who weighed no more than seven or eight pounds."

One reporter asked, "What keeps you going?"

"It's the love of people," he replied. "When we are on our Walk for Hunger through the more populated areas, we talk to perhaps one hundred to two hundred people each day. They embrace us with tears in their eyes when we tell them about hunger."

Then he added, "And it's the love of God that keeps me going. Many, many people have accepted the Lord along the way."

So Bob Wieland's Walk for Hunger has become more than a crusade for starving people. It has turned into an evangelistic endeavor in which a man with no legs is sharing his Christian faith with thousands of people from coast to coast. What a privilege it was to meet this amazing young man and to realize how the Lord has turned a tragic accident in Vietnam into a project that will bring relief from suffering to multitudes of people around the world.

Was the Appearance of a Patrolman a Coincidence?

At a family reunion we had the privilege of attending the other day, there was a discussion about an interesting subject. How often have you experienced what you might call a little miracle when something happens that you can't explain by calling it a *coincidence*! I have had that happen many times, both here at home and in my travels abroad.

I was talking about this to a cousin, Russell Westphal, who makes his living as a carpenter and is the manager of a motel in Osage, Minnesota. He spent a part of his boyhood days in the house where I now live. Folks in this area will remember him for his loyalty to the country church which he attended near his home. Tall and lanky, with a love for story telling and a droll sense of humor, he had something of the manner of Abraham Lincoln. The Mennonites in this community will recall the old folk songs he used to sing to the accompaniment of his guitar at the community Literary Society meetings. One of his favorite songs, as I remember, was entitled "I'm the Guy That Rode the Mule Around the World." How many times he has been asked to sing the hilarious song!

With that introduction, I would like to share the amazing incident he told me of an experience he and his wife Elsie had on a fishing trip into northern Minnesota.

"It's a funny thing," he said, "how many of us could go fishing right in our own backyard, but feel we have to drive a couple hundred miles to the Canadian border to cast out our lines for a mess of fish."

"We had driven most of the day and the sun had almost set." he continued. "We were traveling on a four-lane highway and hadn't seen a patrol car the whole day long. Suddenly, I noticed two motorcyclists pass by me and pull right in front of my car. They were followed by two more cyclists who slowed down beside me. I looked in my rearview mirror and noticed two more of those guys riding side-by-side close behind my car. They had me hemmed in."

"What did they look like," I asked. "Did they look like they could be trusted?"

"They were tough-looking characters with long hair and beards and wore black leather jackets. I began to wonder what they were up to when one of the men signaled to me to pull over to the side of the road. Then I knew what their intentions were. They wanted to relieve me of my wallet. I had about a hundred and fifty dollars and Elsie carried another hundred dollars. We were afraid our house might be broken into, so we carried all of our spare cash with us."

Now comes the miracle. At the very moment when Russ knew he was at the mercy of those six motorcyclists, a

TRUE TALES To Live By

patrol car appeared over the hill on the other side of the interstate.

"The amazing thing was, I hadn't seen a patrol car all day and at the very second I needed him, he appeared," Russell commented.

"What did the patrolman do?" I asked.

"He knew I was in trouble and he headed through the median toward me. Then, you should have seen those cyclists," he added with a chuckle. "They scattered like flies. They drove across the divider ditch and headed back toward the Twin Cities."

"Did you stop to thank the patrolman?" I asked.

"No, I didn't stop. He pulled up behind me but he knew I had no more problems so he turned back. But you can believe I thanked the Lord! And I know this," he added with a smile. "The sudden appearance of that patrolman was no coincidence."

A Veteran Recalls Days on the Battlefield

We had an interesting visit one-day with our long-time friends, Dr. and Mrs. Ed Wafful. He served in the medics during World War II in the Pacific Theater. He told of the fear the soldiers felt when their ship prepared for a landing on a beach in enemy held territory.

As the ramp was lowered at the end of the ship, the soldiers making the attack rushed out to seek cover, often falling flat, face down in the sand, to escape enemy fire. My friend's job was to go ahead of the stretcher-bearers to give first aid to the soldiers who had been wounded.

He recalls that on his first landing, he saw the body of a soldier lying beneath an uprooted tree. He dashed over to see what he could do to help the man who was evidently seriously wounded. Imagine how shocked he was when he pulled aside the branches and saw that the soldier had no head!

He said, "I thought, I can't take this! I'm going to the ship!"

When asked what would have happened had he retreated, he replied, "I'd have been shot."

It would be difficult to picture the bloody slaughter in which the medics, as well as the armed infantry, were involved in a battle. The shells whistling overhead, the cries of the wounded pleading for help. In the midst of this terrible struggle, the medic's task was to bind up the wounds of soldiers whose bodies had been ripped open by shellfire and give first aid until the stretcher-bearers could reach the scene. Our friend sometimes was one of the stretcher-bearers.

This was not a one-day event. Often these landings would go on time after time for several weeks. It's a wonder that the survivors were able to keep their sanity.

He told us this story about how the stretcher- bearers who go out on the battlefield to bring in the wounded and the dead are subject to enemy fire without the protection of foxholes. It is difficult to imagine what death-defying experiences they had to endure with shells bursting all around them.

One would hope that at the end of the day, completely exhausted, they would be able to find a place where they could sleep and get rested up for the next day's trying experience out on the battlefield.

This is a description of how those soldiers found a *restful sleep* at the close of the day. With the shells bursting overhead, they would hurriedly dig a shallow trench back of the front lines. There was no time to dig a deeper one. The trench was dug waist deep. Two men would share it sitting down with knees up to their chests and sleep in that position.

They never dared to put their heads up far enough to look out. If it rained during the night they would often be wet up to their waists. Some men's boots and socks never got dried out and they would get jungle rot in their feet and eventually have to be carried off the field on a stretcher. In this way they tried to get rested for the next day's trying experiences out on the battlefield.

It is no wonder that many of them wished they could get a bullet in the arm or a leg so they could be relieved at least temporarily from their front line duty.

My friend told me an interesting story of one occasion when his unit was transferred to an area where they were released from duty. In their camp, they were assigned to beds. What a relief it must have been, after sleeping in a hurriedly dug trench near the front lines, to have beds in which to sleep, away from the noise of the bursting shells!

One day my friend happened to meet a Filipino who was carrying a monkey on his shoulder. That playful little monkey appealed to him. Reaching in his pocket for a package of cigarettes that were issued to soldiers from time to time, he said, "I'd like to buy your monkey. Will you sell him for a package of cigarettes?"

A moment later he found himself the owner of a monkey that perched comfortably on his shoulder. At night, the monkey's leash was tied to a leg of the bed so he wouldn't escape.

During the week in that camp, that monkey was a good friend of that soldier and no doubt of great interest to the others in the camp. He helped to relieve the pressure of the memory of those horrifying days that they had spent on the battlefront. When the unit was moved to another location, there was a notice circulated among the troops that there would be no animals allowed. My friend sold the monkey to another soldier.

I have related this touching story in the hope that my readers, like myself, will have a deeper appreciation for the American servicemen who went through such almost unbearable experiences so we might have the freedom which we enjoy today.

SKIP WESTPHAL

The Chinese Cake Peddler

On my way to Peru several years ago, I stopped in Key West, Fla., to see a friend of mine who has spent many years as a missionary in China. His father, who had just returned from China, told me a story about a Chinese Cake Peddler.

In the days before the Communist take over in China, a cake peddler in Canton responded to an invitation at an evangelistic meeting, and made the decision to become a Christian and ask for the forgiveness of his sins. As he knelt at the altar, there crept into his heart a feeling of peace and happiness such as he had never known. Rising to his feet, with tears of joy trickling down his cheeks, he exclaimed over and over, "Hallelujah! Hallelujah!"

The following morning, as he started down the street with his tray of cakes, he found that the feeling of peace and joy was still there. Somehow life seemed to be entirely different. The songs of the birds were sweeter than they had been the day before; the flowers were more beautiful and the people he met on the street were friendlier. Perhaps the reason for their friendliness was that the cake peddler greeted them with a happy smile that was not characteristic of him. Some of the folks on the street stopped and stared at him, wondering if some good fortune had come into his life.

As he moved down the street with his cart loaded with cakes, the peddler would call attention to his wares with a melodious chant, "Shao bing ma wha!" (Cakes for sale.) Life seemed so good to the cake peddler this morning that he felt he must add another word to his chant to express his newfound joy. So he added the word, "Hallelujah!"

"Shao bing ma wha! Hallelujah!" the peddler sang at the top of his voice, "Shao bing ma wha! Hallelujah!"

Suddenly a housewife who had been standing in her doorway listening to his chant, stepped out into the street and greeted him.

"Pardon me, my friend," she said. 'For many months I have been buying your tasty cakes. But I am puzzled. What is this 'Hallelujah' you have to sell?"

"Would you like some of it?" the peddler inquired with an eager smile.

"Why, yes," the lady replied. "If it's as good as your cake. Yes, I'd like some."

"My dear lady," replied the peddler, "this 'Hallelujah' isn't for sale. It's an expression of joy about something that happened to me last night."

Then he related to her his wonderful experience of the previous night. Encouraged by her deep interest in his story, he invited her to pray with him and to invite the Lord Jesus into her heart. The lady was so moved by the cake peddler's testimony that she knelt down in the street and prayed for the forgiveness of her sins. As she prayed, she too, felt happiness in her heart like that which the cake peddler had described.

The peddler was so overjoyed at the housewife's response, that he resolved to continue this unusual method of witnessing to his religious experience. As he pushed his cake cart down the street, he continued to call out, "Shao bing ma wha! Hallelujah! Shao bing ma wha! Hallelujah!"

Like the housewife, others inquired about the meaning of the word, "Hallelujah!" and each time the cake peddler used that opportunity to tell the happy story about how he had met the Lord. During the days that followed, many of the people who lived on the streets which his route covered were led to the Lord through the eager witness of this enthusiastic Christian and his street cry of, "Shao bing ma wha! Hallelujah!"

Home from Peru on Crutches

I was in Key West, Florida, as I had been asked to accompany a friend of mine to lead the singing on an evangelistic tour

SKIP WESTPHAL

in Peru. That was when I heard the story of the Chinese Cake Peddler. I have shared that inspiring story many times in Iowa and surrounding States.

At the last moment, due to some unexpected problems in his church, my friend had to cancel out on the trip. I decided that since I had come this far, I would go on the trip to Peru by myself. Perhaps I could get some stories about which I could write in my newspaper column or in a magazine story.

One of my interesting experiences in Peru was to visit a fishmeal factory in Chimbote. I knew that fishmeal was used extensively in the United States in feed for sheep and cattle.

I had climbed a ladder to get a photograph of an elevator that was moving the fishmeal to another bin. Suddenly, the platform on which I was standing gave way and I fell ten feet on my back to the floor below. Workers at the factory carried me to a taxi and the driver took me to a hospital. My fall had resulted in a fractured pelvis, but this was not found by the x-rays.

While in the hospital, I had a visitor who told me he had a friend who was killed in that same kind of fall. I was told by my doctor in the hospital that there were no funeral homes in Chimbote and it was a law in that city that a person who dies there had to be buried within twenty-four hours.

Who would have notified Marion if I had been killed in the fall? I could have been buried in Chimbote and she might not have heard about it until many days later. What a heart breaking tragedy we escaped! How thankful we were to our Good Lord for watching over me in that trying experience.

My roommate during my stay at the hospital was an English sailor who had to have surgery due to complications caused by a burst appendix. He helped me to the bathroom everyday, as I was unable to walk due to my pelvis injury.

I had with me a copy of a Gideon New Testament. During my stay at the hospital, my roommate told me that he had read the four Gospels.

He said, "Won't my shipmates be surprised when they see me reading my New Testament during our spare time between ports."

After three weeks, I was sufficiently recovered that I was able to use crutches to board a plane and head for home. When my plane arrived at Des Moines, Marion and my two daughters, Kim and Sunia, were waiting for me at the airport. As I disembarked from the plane and got into the wheelchair they had waiting for me, I threw my arms around them and exclaimed, "This time I almost didn't make it." I resolved never again to leave on a trip without my family.

On my arrival home, my doctor put me to bed at home for six weeks to recover from my injury—which proved by x-rays here to be a fractured pelvis.

Marion had been starting to cultivate the corn and beans, and although she had done much field work, she hadn't had the experience of cultivating. It was quite a worrisome problem for her.

One morning she looked out of the window and reported excitedly, "Skip, there is a whole string of tractors coming down the road. There must be eight or ten of them."

A moment later she added, "They are turning in at our gate and they have cultivators on them! They must be coming to cultivate our crop!"

That's what they were about to do. In a few hours they had finished the job which would have taken Marion several days. These neighbors were our Mennonite neighbors. In all of my farming experience, I have never seen such an outpouring of friendly neighborliness as I did that day.

If I hadn't made that trip to Peru and met that Christian missionary, what an inspiring story I would have missed. I have told it over and over, the experience of the cake peddler who with one word, led many of his Chinese friends to find the Lord.

The "Good Doctor" of Lambarene

The impact which the "Good Doctor" from Lambarene has made on the hearts of the American people, and on the lives of millions of men, women and children throughout the world is immeasurable. There is probably no living man who is held in deeper respect by people everywhere than Dr. Schweitzer. He is truly one of the greatest gifts Africa has made to modern life—more important than all the gold and diamonds on the entire continent.

I recall the time I delivered an illustrated lecture on Africa to a group of school children in Mason City, Iowa. I had thought that these young people would be more interested in stories about lions and snakes and elephants than in Dr. Schweitzer, so I referred only briefly to a visit I had made to Lambarene. At the conclusion of my lecture, the first question these teen-age youngsters asked was this: "Can you tell us more about Dr. Schweitzer?"

On my third trip to Africa, I resolved to make an attempt to meet this man who has captured the imagination of the entire world. I was in Nairobi, Kenya, when I wrote Dr. Schweitzer, asking if he would consent to a brief interview. Several weeks passed without a reply, no doubt due to the fact that he was usually months behind in his correspondence.

TRUE TALES To Live By

The time finally came for me to return to New York, and I decided to plan my trip home by way of Lambarene, hoping that I might be able to see Dr. Schweitzer, even if only for a few minutes.

On my arrival by plane at Lambarene, I checked in at a little hotel in the village. Then I hired an African with a canoe to take me down the river about two miles to the hospital of Dr. Schweitzer.

When I reached the hospital, I was greeted very cordially by one of the nurses, who took me immediately to Dr. Schweitzer. He was at work in his laboratory, but told the nurse he would see me in a few minutes. In the meantime, the nurse introduced me to Mrs. Schweitzer, who led the way to their home in one wing of the hospital and informed me that I was most welcome at Lambarene. She was the gracious, kindly person I had always pictured her to be.

In a few moments, Dr. Schweitzer appeared, a distinguished looking gentleman with grey mustache, unruly hair, and a kindly manner that set one immediately at ease. When he learned that I had checked in at the hotel, he insisted that I must be his guest. I shall always remember the friendly twinkle in his eyes as he stood with his hand on my shoulder welcoming me to Lambarene.

After visiting for a few minutes, the doctor sat down at his desk and penned a note to the manager of my hotel, informing him that the American visitor was to be his guest. Then he called for three of his native boys to get their paddles and take me in his boat to the hotel to call for my luggage.

It was almost dark when we returned to the hospital. Standing on the shore with a lantern was one of the nurses, waiting for us. She had been worried for fear we would be caught in a thunderstorm. It was very dangerous, they said, to be out on the river during a storm.

As we walked up the path leading to the staff quarters—the nurse leading the way with the lantern—we passed below a window where Dr. Schweitzer was bent over a desk, busily at work. She called out to him that we had returned safely.

"Dr. Schweitzer is always concerned about his guests," she said. "He feels that he is responsible for their comfort and their safety."

"The doctor is working rather late," I remarked.

"He always works late," she replied. "He starts at seven in the morning and works until eleven at night. This goes on every day, with never time off for a holiday."

Dr. Schweitzer's staff consisted of two surgeons and ten nurses. There were usually six or eight other Europeans who did general supervisory work about the hospital grounds. The nurses did not receive, nor did they expect, any salary. Their only monetary remuneration was a few dollars a week pocket money.

All the members of the staff had their meals together in a large dining hall. At dinner that night, a group of children from the leper colony sang outside the dining room window. They were serenading one of the nurses, Miss Balsiger, who was returning to Switzerland the next day after two and a half years of service in Lambarene. Their song, which they sang very beautifully, was that well loved old hymn, "Take the Name of Jesus with You."

After the dishes had been cleared away, Dr. Schweitzer rose and made a few remarks, thanking Miss Balsiger for all her kindness to the leper patients she had ministered to so faithfully, and expressing the hope that one day she would return to Lambarene. Then he walked over to the piano and led in the singing of a German hymn. After the singing, he returned to his place at the table and read a passage from the Bible, concluding with the Lord's Prayer. This was a daily custom at Lambarene.

It was evident that Dr. Schweitzer enjoyed being with people. He took a great interest in his guests, inquiring about the purpose of their trip and how they had been enjoying their travels in Africa. He loved to tell stories and had a delightful sense of humor.

TRUE TALES To Live By

One day at the dinner table, he made a remark to one of the nurses about the stupidity of his dog, Choo-choo.

"Oh, but he is good!" the nurse remonstrated.

"The stupid can also be good," replied Dr. Schweitzer. Then with a twinkle in his eyes and pointing to himself, he chuckled, "I know—from experience!"

After breakfast on the second day of my visit, there was a knock at my door. It was Dr. Schweitzer. He had come to invite me to accompany him on a walk through his orchard to check on the work the natives were doing in preparation for the planting of new fruit trees.

It was a most interesting experience, listening to the doctor advising the workers about how the job should be done and observing the look of pride on his face as he pointed out the beautiful trees he had planted with his own hands. He said that he and one of the nurses, Miss Kottmann, had planted about a thousand fruit trees— mostly grapefruit, tangerines, lemons, and oranges—during the past thirty years. The patients may eat as much of the fruit as they wish, he said, but they are not permitted to sell it.

To prepare the soil for planting, holes were dug by the leper patients who were able to work. Into these holes was thrown all the refuse—banana peelings, dead leaves, discarded food—all the waste from the hospital. After about six months, this refuse had turned into rich, black soil that was carried in boxes by the natives and dumped into holes six feet deep and six feet in diameter. Into this fertile soil the new trees were planted.

All day long there was a bustle of activity at the hospital. All the patients who were able to work were kept busy washing the linen, cleaning the rooms, working in the orchard. This was a happy arrangement for it made the time pass more quickly. The value of work was especially noticeable among the leper patients who were very depressed on Sundays when there was no work to do.

Many of the patients had to travel great distances to have their health restored by the healing hand of the beloved doctor. Some of them made a journey of two or three weeks by canoe to reach the hospital. As they were usually too ill to paddle their own pirogue, a member of the family accompanied them. They brought with them chickens, ducks, and goats—the ducks for food, the hens to provide them with eggs. They brought their goats along as they were fearful that the animals would be stolen if they left them at home. There were a hundred or more goats running about the hospital village.

Each family did its own cooking, as the natives represented fifteen or twenty different tribes, and they had a fear of being poisoned if their food was cooked by someone other than their own tribesmen.

One feature of Dr. Schweitzer's hospital that delighted both the staff and the patients was his collection of pets. Formerly, the natives killed wild animals for food and permitted the young ones to die of starvation. They knew that the good doctor did not approve of this so they brought the babies to him. There were living at the hospital village quite a number of the wild creatures of the woods, including several antelope, a chimpanzee and a baby gorilla.

It is difficult to estimate the blessing Dr. Schweitzer was to the people of Africa—the thousands of lives he had saved, the suffering he alleviated, the new hope he gave to despairing hearts.

It is to the lepers that he probably rendered the greatest service. Due to the recent discovery of new drugs, that horrible disease could now be checked if it was treated in its early stages. There were still those who delayed too long, such as a child we saw at the leper village who had lost all her fingers to the disease. She was a pathetic sight as she sat on a bench by the door of one of the huts, trying to learn to sew with the stubs that remained of her fingers.

Before the good doctor came with his healing drugs, a leper was doomed to years of disgrace and suffering from this loathsome disease. His former friends, and even the members of his family refused to associate with him. A lingering death was the only hope of relieving his misery. A miracle was being wrought at Lambarene. Lepers were being cleansed.

From far and wide they came—men, women and children, traveling painfully for many days along the forest trails and up the turbulent rivers in their tiny canoes. They came like slaves who were yearning for freedom—freedom from a disease that was more to be dreaded than even the bonds of slavery.

Dr. Schweitzer crossed the seas to minister to the needs of the people in the jungle country of French Equatorial Africa. Yet his greatest influence for good has been outside of Africa, among people of other countries. Several thousand people in Africa have felt the touch of his healing hand, but many millions of men, women, and children in other parts of the world have been inspired by his example of love and his unselfish devotion to the task of relieving human suffering.

The *Good Doctor* now has gone to be with the Lord but he will live on in the hearts of millions of people around the world.

When asked why he left the comforts of civilization to minister to primitive people in that, faraway land, his answer was three words I shall never forget. He said, "Jesus sent me."

The Stranger on the Moscow Subway

When I visited the Red Square in Moscow several years ago, I had the opportunity to enter the tomb, or vault, where Lenin and Stalin were on display for the public to see. It was an eerie feeling to look upon the face of Stalin, the man who had been responsible for the murder of millions of his fellow countrymen.

I had another experience in Moscow which was much more inspiring than the sight of the infamous Russian murderer lying in his coffin. I wanted to get to the National

Hotel to see a friend of mine who had just arrived from New York City. I was attempting to explain to the lady at the subway ticket window where I wished to go, but she couldn't understand me.

I had almost given up in frustration when a stranger approached me and said in a halting tone of voice, "National Hotel? Come. I will show you."

I had been warned about trusting Russian strangers in Moscow, but the man seemed so friendly that I decided to take a chance. Rather hesitatingly, I followed him down the steps into a waiting subway car. The stranger carried in his hand two bouquets of orange blossoms. As a gesture of friendship, he insisted that I take one of them.

"You American—me Russian," he said. "We must be friends."

I heartily agreed with him, but we were unable to carry on much of a conversation because of our language barrier.

At the third stop, he motioned for me to follow him out of the car and up the stairs to the subway exit. In spite of the man's friendliness, I was still wondering if I was being a bit gullible.

When we emerged from the subway, my friend pointed to the lights of the National Hotel nearby. Since he had gone out of his way to help me, I felt that I should give him something to show my appreciation. All I could find in my pockets in the way of a souvenir was a buffalo nickel, one of the coins I gave to Russian children now and then. He thanked me for the souvenir; then he started searching through the pockets of his rather threadbare looking coat for something to give me. Finally he came up with a piece of paper. Then he asked for a loan of my pen and wrote something on the paper.

Handing me my pen and the paper, he bowed slightly, said goodbye in Russian and disappeared in the crowd. I looked at the paper and was amazed to see that it was a ten ruble note which at that time, was worth about $2.50 in American money. Then I glanced at the words he had written on the note and was surprised to see that they were written in English. "I love de Amerikans."

I stared at the words for a few moments in disbelief, then I called out to him but he had disappeared in the crowd. Often I wished that I had his name and address so I could have written him to express my appreciation for his friendliness. I am sure I will never see him again, but that experience on a street corner in Moscow, and other similar contacts I had later, have led me to believe that most of the so-called *common people* of Russia are, at heart, yearning for the friendship of the American people.

STORIES THAT TOUCH THE HEART

SKIP WESTPHAL

A Shepherd Calling His Lost Sheep

Recently I heard a story of a shepherd and his family who lived in the highlands of Scotland. I think it is worthy to appear in this book. I am interested in stories of sheep, for we once raised sheep here on Dun Rovin' Farm. At one time we had a flock of twenty ewes, and at lambing time the number would be increased to some fifty sheep. We raised pedigree dogs, too, and one day I counted fifty-five puppies in our kennels at Dun Rovin' Farm. Life was humming with activity here in those days.

Our two daughters were around eight years old then and they helped take care of the dogs and the sheep. Quite often there would be an orphan lamb that was not accepted by the mother and had to be bottle-fed. What an interesting sight it was to see the little lamb scampering across the barnyard when one of the girls poked the milk bottle through the back gate and called for him to come and get his lunch!

Often one of the girls would come running from the barn calling out excitedly, "We've got another pair of twins! Another pair of twins!"

Now and then we were even blessed with triplets. I recall on one occasion, Herb Plambeck, an international traveler, was the guest speaker at a commencement program in Palmer, Iowa, and we invited him to spend the night at our home. We told him about our new triplets that we had named Tom, Dick and Harriet. He was so amused by the names that on his noon broadcast the next day he told about how he had been entertained at a farm home near Palmer, and of how the family was celebrating the arrival of triplet lambs named Tom, Dick and Harriet.

But to get to the story, usually in the morning after enjoying their tea and scones, the Scotsman and his young daughter would go out in the hills back of his house and call the sheep to come in for their feed. Sometimes the daughter

197

would give the sheep call and the ewes with their lambs came streaming in to get their breakfast.

The time came when the shepherd's daughter went away to school in Edinburgh. At first she wrote home often; then the letters became less frequent. The shepherd and his wife became very worried.

One day they heard through a friend that their daughter wasn't living the kind of life which her Christian parents had taught her; that she was in some kind of trouble. Deeply concerned, the father decided to go to Edinburgh to visit her.

When he called at the address from which she had written, he was told she didn't live there anymore. He called at the school, and learned she was no longer a student there. For hours he searched for his missing daughter, but without success. Finally he decided he would try a method he had often used when searching for lost sheep—the call of the shepherd. Passersby stood and stared in amazement as the bearded gentleman in the shepherd's clothes lifted his voice in a strange call never before heard on these city streets… "Sheeeep! Sheeeep!" No doubt everyone thought the man was *addled in the head.*

Up one street and down another, he slowly made his way with the call of the shepherd for his sheep. (I visited Edinburgh years ago and I can see in my mind's eye those picturesque city streets.) Finally the shepherd found himself in the slum section of the city which was populated by some unsavory characters. "Surely," he thought, "I won't find my daughter here!" He was about to turn and leave when he decided to make one more try. His heart would have ached had he known the circumstances under which his daughter was living on this very street. He almost hoped she would not be found in this disreputable part of the city.

Summing up his courage, he lifted his voice again in the shepherd's call. This time his daughter heard that familiar sound.

Sitting up in bed, she exclaimed, "What am I hearing? I must be imagining this!"

But then it came again, echoing up the cobblestone streets, the call she had so often heard in the highlands back home. Jumping from her bed, she quickly dressed and dashed down the stairs. As she opened the door, there just a few steps away on a street corner, stood the familiar figure of her father. She ran to him and threw her arms about his neck as tears streamed down the faces of the father and his long-lost daughter. The sheep's call had found her.

The conclusion of the story is that the daughter returned home with her father, and from then on her life was changed. She once again became the kind of person of whom her parents were very proud. The tears come to my eyes as I write this touching story. How much it reminds us of the story of *The Prodigal Son*.

Saved By a Smile

A soldier by the name of Saint-Exupery tells of an unusual experience when he fought in the Civil War against the Fascists.

He said that he was captured by the enemy and thrown into a jail cell. He was sure that from the contemptuous looks and rough treatment he received from his jailers he would be executed the next day.

I'll tell the story as I remember it. He wrote, "I was sure that I was to be killed. I became terribly nervous and distraught. I fumbled in my pockets to see if there were any cigarettes that had escaped their search. I found one and because of my shaking hands, I could barely get it to my lips. But I had no matches. They had taken those. I looked through the bars at my jailer. He did not make eye contact with me. After all, one does not make eye contact with a thing, a corpse.

"I called out to him, 'Have you got a light, por favor?' He looked at me and shrugged and came over to light my cigarette. As he came close and lit the match, his eyes inadvertently locked with mine. At that moment, I smiled. I don't know why I did that. Perhaps it was nervousness, perhaps it was because, when you get very close, one to another, it is very hard not to smile. In any case, I smiled.

"In that instant, it was as a spark jumped across the gap between our two hearts, our two human souls. I know he didn't want to, but my smile leaped through the bars and generated a smile on his lips, too. He lit my cigarette but stayed near, looking at me directly in the eyes and continuing to smile.

"I kept smiling at him, now aware of him as a person and not just a jailer. And his looking at me seemed to have a new dimension, too. 'Do you have kids?' he asked.

"'Yes, here, here.' I took out my wallet and nervously fumbled for the pictures of my family. He, too, took out the pictures of his children and began to talk about his plans and hopes for them. My eyes filled with tears. I said that I feared that I'd never see my family again, never have the chance to see them grow up. Tears came to his eyes, too.

"Suddenly, without another word, he unlocked my cell and silently led me out. Out of the jail, quietly and by back routes, out of the town. There at the edge of town, he released me. And without another word, he turned back toward the town.

"My life was saved by a smile."

I Want To Buy a Miracle

Sally was only eight years old when she heard Mommy and Daddy talking about her little brother, Georgi. He was very sick and they had done everything they could afford to save his life. Only a very expensive surgery could help him now...and that was out of the financial question. She heard Daddy say it with a whispered desperation, "Only a miracle can save him now."

SKIP WESTPHAL

Sally went to her bedroom and pulled her piggybank from its hiding place in the closet. She shook all the change out on the floor and counted it carefully. Three times. The total had to be exactly perfect. No chance here for mistakes. Tying the coins up in a cold-weather handkerchief, she slipped out of the apartment and made her way to the corner drug store.

She waited patiently for the pharmacist to give her attention, but he was too busy talking to another man to be bothered by an eight-year-old. Sally twisted her feet to make a scuffing noise. She cleared her throat. No good. Finally she took a quarter from its hiding place and banged it on the glass counter. That did it!

"And what do you want?" the pharmacist asked in an annoyed tone of voice. "I'm talking to my brother."

"Well, I want to talk to you about my brother," Sally answered back in the same annoyed tone. "He's sick...and I want to buy a miracle."

"I beg your pardon," said the pharmacist.

"My Daddy says only a miracle can save him now...so how much does a miracle cost?"

"We don't sell miracles here, little girl. I can't help you."

"Listen, I have the money to pay for it. Just tell me how much it costs."

A well-dressed man standing nearby heard the conversation between the little girl and the pharmacist and asked. "What kind of a miracle does your brother need?"

"I don't know," Sally answered. A tear started down her cheek. "I just know he's really sick and Mommy says he needs an operation. But my folks can't pay for it...so I have my money."

"How much do you have?" asked the well-dressed man.

"A dollar and eleven cents," Sally answered proudly. "And it's all the money I have in the world."

TRUE TALES To Live By

"Well, what a coincidence," smiled the well-dressed man. "A dollar and eleven cents...the exact price of a miracle to save a little brother."

He took her money in one hand and with the other hand he grasped her mitten and said, "Take me to where you live. I want to see your brother and meet your parents."

That well-dressed man was Dr. Carlton Armstrong, renowned surgeon who specialized in the malady that Georgi had. The operation was completed without charge and it wasn't long until Georgi was home again and doing well. Mommy and Daddy were happily talking about the chain of events that had led them to this place.

"That surgery," Mommy whispered. "It's a miracle. I wonder how much it would have cost?"

Sally smiled to herself. She knew exactly how much a miracle cost—one dollar and eleven cents, plus the faith of a little child.

A Boy's Sense of Humor

Part of the fun of being associated with boys is in observing the names they give to themselves and their pets.

Four of the most interesting years of my life were spent as the associate director of the Golden Rule Farm for Boys in Franklin, New Hampshire. The names the boys gave to each other and to their pets intrigued me.

An eight-year-old boy named Shotgun Shorty had three pet ducks. He called them Donald, Sebastian, and Heliotrope. I have no idea where he got those unusual names for his ducks except Donald, and I think he didn't know either. I can't explain why his friends called him Shotgun Shorty. At his age, I'm sure he never carried a shotgun.

Another one of the boys was quite small for his age. He went by the name of Spanky Pee Wee Joslyn. His pets for a while were three little kittens named Shadrach, Meshak, and Abednego. I'm sure he got those names from the Bible Story he heard in Sunday School about the three children who survived the miraculous experience of existing in a fiery furnace.

Georgie Porgie Brown wasn't much interested in kittens or ducks. He had a pet pig that went by the unusual name of Philip. When asked why he gave that name to his pet pig, he replied with a grin, "Cause he's so hard to fill up!"

What If the Lady Had Caught that Bus

A new pastor was assigned to reopen an old church in Brooklyn, New York. When he and his family arrived, they were a bit discouraged to find the building badly in need of repair. They went to work, spending days, with the help of some former parishioners. After several days they had the church ready to reopen.

Then on December 19, a driving rainstorm struck the church. To the dismay of the pastor and his wife, the roof leaked so badly that a large chunk of plaster broke loose and fell just behind the pulpit, leaving a huge hole about six feet across. The Christmas service would have to be postponed.

On the way home, the pastor noticed that a local business was having a flea market type sale for charity so he stopped in. One of the items was a beautiful handmade, ivory colored, crocheted tablecloth with exquisite work, fine colors and a cross embroidered right in the center. It was just the right size to cover up the hole in the front wall. He bought it and headed back to the church. By this time, it had started to snow. The pastor noticed an older woman running by the church trying to catch a bus. She missed it so the pastor invited her to wait in the warm church for the next bus forty-five minutes later.

TRUE TALES To Live By

She sat in a pew and paid no attention to the pastor while he got a ladder, hangers, etc., to put up the tablecloth as a wall tapestry. The pastor could hardly believe how beautiful it looked and it covered up the entire problem area. Then he noticed the woman walking down the center aisle. Her face was like a sheet.

"Pastor," she asked, "Where did you get that tablecloth?" The pastor explained. The woman asked him to check the lower right corner to see if the initials EBG were crocheted into it there. They were. These were the initials of the woman, and she had made this tablecloth thirty-five years before.

The woman could hardly believe it as the pastor told how he had just gotten the tablecloth. The woman explained that before the war she and her husband were well-to-do people in Austria. When the Nazis came, she was forced to leave. Her husband was going to follow her the next week. He was captured, sent to prison and she never saw her husband or her home again.

The pastor wanted to give her the tablecloth; but she insisted he keep it for the church. He offered to drive her home. She lived on the other side of Staten Island and was only in Brooklyn for the day for a house-cleaning job.

What a wonderful service they had on Christmas Eve. The church was almost full. The music and the spirit were great. At the end of the service, the pastor and his wife greeted everyone at the door and many said that they would return. One older man, whom the pastor recognized from the neighborhood, continued to sit in the pew and stare, and the pastor wondered why he wasn't leaving. The man asked him where he got the tablecloth on the front wall because it was identical to the one that his wife had made years ago when they lived in Austria, before the war. How could there be two tablecloths so much alike?

He told the pastor how the Nazis came, how he forced his wife to flee for her safety, and how he was supposed to follow her, but he was arrested and put in a concentration camp. He never saw his wife or his home again for all those thirty-five years.

The pastor could hardly contain himself for excitement as he offered to take him for a little ride. He and his wife drove to Staten Island and to the same house where the pastor had taken the woman three days earlier. He helped the man climb the three flights of stairs to the woman's apartment and knocked on the door. When the lady opened it, the pastor and his wife saw the greatest Christmas reunion they could ever have imagined.

John Wayne's Response to a Young Girl's Letter

A friend of mine shared with me a story. It's about a young lady, Cindy Schuller, daughter of well-known TV minister Robert Schuller. One day while on a trip overseas she was involved in a motorcycle accident. I remember reading about it in the news. It was feared at first that the accident would be fatal but she finally recovered except that she had to have one of her legs amputated.

John Wayne was a fan of Robert Schuller and when he saw a newspaper story about Cindy's accident he wrote a note to Cindy. It read:

> Dear Cindy,
>
> Sorry to hear about your accident. Hope you get to be all right.
>
> Signed, John Wayne

Cindy was so pleased to receive a letter from the famous movie actor that she wrote Wayne a note in reply. Following is a copy of her letter to John Wayne:

TRUE TALES To Live By

Dear Mr. Wayne,

I got your note. Thanks for writing to me. I like you very much. I am going to be all right because Jesus is going to help me. Mr. Wayne do you know Jesus? I sure hope you do, Mr. Wayne, because I cannot imagine heaven being complete without John Wayne being there. If you don't know Jesus I hope that you will give your heart to Him right now. See you in Heaven.

Signed, Cindy

Cindy asked a friend of Wayne's to give her note to him. It just happened that her friend met Wayne at a dinner party the following night. It had become well known that the movie actor was suffering from cancer and had not long to live. The dinner party was in his honor. During the party everyone was laughing and cutting up when his friend, who gave Wayne the letter, noticed he was crying.

He asked him, "Hey Duke, what's the matter?"

Wayne put the letter in his pocket and pointed to his friend who had delivered it to him and said, "You go tell that little girl, that right here, in this restaurant, right now, I have accepted Christ and will meet her one day in heaven."

Three weeks later, on Monday, June 11, 1979, the Duke died of cancer. John Wayne was widely respected for his western heritage values and personal integrity.

The Handwriting on the Wall

Le occasion es corno el fiereno; se ha de marchacar caliente."

Martin Fierrio

One day while browsing around a little gift shop in Buenos Aires, South America, I noticed a quotation printed on a strip of leather as a wall motto. Translated, it means, "The occasion is as steel; one must strike while the iron is hot."

I came across that incident the other day when I was looking through some of my notes I had completely forgotten about. How I happened to be in Buenos Aires so many years ago was that I had just been released from two weeks in a hospital, recovering from phlebitis due to the bite of a poisonous snake in Africa. I was waiting for the next ship to Boston. That was about fifty years ago.

Isn't it interesting to note that when I saw that quotation in Spanish I might have just walked by without giving a thought to what those words meant. Why did I bother to ask the proprietor of the store to translate it for me? I had no idea that fifty years later I would use that quotation in an article for the *Fort Dodge Messenger*. Isn't it true that the hand of the Good Lord is always with us no matter where we are, giving us the urge to do something that may seem inconsequential at the time.

Let's think for a moment about the words of that Spanish quotation. A blacksmith knows that he can't do a thing with a piece of cold steel, no matter how hard he strikes it with his hammer. But when the steel is hot, he can bend it and form it into all kinds of shapes, even beautiful ornamental designs.

Isn't it true in our lives that there are occasions when we have the urge to do something, perhaps write a letter or make a phone call to a friend who is desperately in need of encouragement, but we procrastinate and put it off and never get it done. We should have struck while the iron was hot.

That thought came to my mind yesterday when I came across a poem entitled, *The Handwriting on the Wall*. Suppose the mother in that poem had just given vent to her anger at her little son, possibly punishing him for what he had done and never really forgiven him. This poem would never have been written. But she felt a loving urge to overlook his careless art. She yielded to the urge while the iron was hot, and loved her son for what he had done. What a beautiful poem resulted from it!

TRUE TALES To Live By

The Handwriting on the Wall

A weary mother returned from the store,
Lugging groceries through the kitchen door.
Awaiting her arrival was her eight-year-old son,
Anxious to relate what his younger brother had done.

"While I was out playing and Dad was on a call,
T.J. took his crayons and wrote on the wall!
It's on the new paper you just hung in the den.
I told him you'd be mad at having to do it again.

She let out a moan and furrowed her brow,
"Where is your little brother right now?"
She emptied her arms and with a purposeful stride,
She marched to his closet where he had gone to hide.

She called his name as she entered the room.
He trembled with fear—he knew that meant doom!
For the next ten minutes, she ranted and raved
About the expensive wallpaper, and how she had saved.

Lamenting all the work it would take to repair,
She condemned his actions and total lack of care.
Then stomped from his room totally distraught!

She headed for the den to confirm her fears
When she saw the wall, her eyes flooded with tears.
The message she read pierced her soul with a dart.
It said, "I love Mommy," surrounded by a heart.

Well the wallpaper remained, just as she found it,
With an empty picture frame hung to surround it.
A reminder to her and indeed to all
Take time to read the handwriting on the wall.

SKIP WESTPHAL

The Little Girl at the Window

Since I was a boy, I have loved a poem written by the *Hoosier poet*, James Whitcomb Riley. One day while on a trip to Boston, I stopped to visit his birthplace in Greenfield, Indiana.

In the center of the town was a monument to the famous poet. As I stood there looking at the monument, I noticed a boy and a little girl standing there, holding hands and admiring the monument. Said the boy to the girl, "Who is your favorite poet?"

The girl, with deep admiration replied slowly, "James Whitcomb Riley."

That incident happened over sixty years ago and I still remember it.

The value of a smile is beautifully illustrated in a story that is told about the famous Evangelist Charles Spurgeon. He was so popular as a preacher that a huge tabernacle was built in London to hold his huge audiences.

One day Dwight Moody visited Spurgeon's church. When he was asked what he thought of Spurgeon, he said, "He is a perpetual stream of Christian sunlight," said Mr. Moody, explaining with a story.

One Sunday in London, Spurgeon said to Moody, just before he commenced his sermon, "Moody, I want you to notice that family there in one of the front seats, and when we go home I want to tell you their story."

When they got home, Spurgeon told Moody that all in that family were won by a smile. When Moody questioned how that could be, Spurgeon explained,

"As I was walking down a street one day, I saw a child at a window. The child smiled, and I smiled, and we bowed. It was the same the second time. I bowed; she bowed. It was not long before there was another child, and I had gotten into the habit of looking and bowing, and pretty soon the group grew, and at last, as I went by, a lady was with them. I didn't know what to do. I didn't want to bow to her,

TRUE TALES To Live By

but I knew the children expected it, and so I bowed to them all. The mother saw I was a minister, because I carried a Bible every Sunday morning. So the children followed me the next Sunday and found I was a minister. And they thought I was the greatest preacher, and their parents must hear me. A minister who is kind to a child and gives him a pat on the head, why, the children will think he is the greatest preacher in the world. Kindness goes a great way. And, finally, the father and mother and five children were converted, and they are going to join our church next Sunday."

We must get the wrinkles out of our brows, and we must have smiling faces, if we want to succeed in our work of love.

A Surprise Christmas Gift

It was the Christmas season. The beautiful lights decorated the homes; people were busy Christmas shopping, and the Salvation Army was ringing its bells to remind us that part of celebrating the birthday of our Lord Jesus is to give gifts, not only to our families and friends, but to those in need.

The story we are about to share with our readers is a beautiful illustration of this truth. It is one of those true tales that warm the heart.

In September 1960, a mother woke up one morning with six hungry children and just seventy-five cents in her pocket. The father was gone. The boys ranged in age from three months to seven years; their sister was two. Their dad had never been much more than a presence they feared. Whenever they heard his tires crunch on the gravel driveway they would scramble to hide under their beds. He did manage to leave fifteen dollars a week to get groceries. Now that he had decided to leave, there would be no more beatings, but no food either.

SKIP WESTPHAL

If there was a welfare system in effect in southern Indiana at that time, the mother certainly knew nothing about it. She scrubbed the kids until they looked brand new and then put on her best homemade dress. She loaded them into the rusty old '51 Chevy and drove off to find a job. The seven of them went to every factory, store and restaurant in their small town. No luck. The children stayed, crammed into the car, and tried to be quiet while she tried to convince whoever would listen that she was willing to learn or do anything. She just had to have a job. Still no luck!

The last place she went to, just a few miles out of town, was an old Root Beer Barrel drive-in that had been converted to a truck stop. It was called the Big Wheel. An old lady named Granny owned the place and she peeked out of the window from time to time at all those kids. She needed someone on the graveyard shift—eleven at night until seven in the morning. She paid sixty-five cents an hour, and she would let her start that night.

The mother raced home and called the teenager down the street that babysat for people. She bargained with her to come and sleep on her sofa for a dollar a night.

She could arrive with her pajamas on and the kids would already be asleep. This seemed like a good arrangement to her, so they made it a deal. That night when the little ones and the mother knelt to say their prayers, they all thanked God for finding mommy a job. And so she started at the Big Wheel. When she got home in the mornings, she woke the babysitter up and sent her home with one dollar of her tip money, fully half of what she averaged every night.

As the weeks went by, heating bills added another strain to her meager wage. The tires on the old Chevy had the consistency of penny balloons and began to leak. She had to fill them with air on the way to work and again every morning before she could go home. One bleak fall morning, she dragged herself to her car to go home and found four tires in the back seat. New tires! There was no note, no nothing, just those beautiful brand new tires. Had angels taken up residence in Indiana, she wondered?

She made a deal with the owner of the local service station. In exchange for his mounting her new tires, she would clean up his office. It took her a lot longer to scrub his floor than it did for him to do the tires. She was now working six nights instead of five a week and it still wasn't enough.

Christmas was coming and she knew there would be no money for toys for the kids. She found a can of red paint and started repairing and painting some old toys. Then she hid them in the basement so there would be something for Santa to deliver on Christmas morning. Clothes were a worry, too. She was sewing patches on top of patches on the boy's pants, and soon they would be too far-gone to repair.

On Christmas Eve the usual customers were drinking coffee in the Big Wheel. There were the truckers, Les, Frank, and Jim, and a state trooper named Joe. The regulars all just sat around and talked through the wee hours of the morning and then left to get home before the sun came up.

When it was time for her to go home at seven o'clock on Christmas morning, she hurried to the car. She was hoping the kids wouldn't wake up before she could manage to get home, and get the presents from the basement placed under the tree, (they had cut down a small cedar tree by the side of the road down by the dump.) It was still dark and she couldn't see much, but there appeared to be some dark shadows in the car—or was that just a trick of the night? Something certainly looked different, but it was hard to tell what.

She peered warily into one of the side windows. Then her jaw dropped in amazement. The old battered Chevy was full—full to the top with boxes of all shapes and sizes. She quickly opened the driver's side door, scrambled inside, and kneeled on the front seat to peer into the back. Reaching back she pulled off the lid of the top box. Inside was a whole case of little blue jeans, sizes two through ten! She looked inside another box. It was full of shirts to go with the jeans. Then she peeked inside some of the other boxes. There was candy and nuts and bananas and bags of groceries. There was an enormous ham for baking, and canned vegetables and potatoes. There was a whole bag of laundry supplies and cleaning items. And there were five toy trucks and one beautiful little doll."

As she drove back through empty streets with the sun coming up on the most amazing Christmas Day of her life, she was sobbing with gratitude. And she never forget the joy on the faces of her little ones that precious morning.

Yes, there were some friendly people that long ago Christmas who cared for the woman and her children, and they all hung out at the Big Wheel Truck Stop."

This Is Jim Checking In

This poem is a heartwarming one and is appropriate for any season of the year.

A minister passing through his church in the middle of the day
Decided to pause by the altar and see who had come to pray.
Just then the back door opened, a man came down the aisle.
The minister frowned as he saw the man hadn't shaved in awhile.
His shirt was kinda' shabby and his coat was worn and frayed.
The man knelt, he bowed his head, then rose and walked away.

In the days that followed, each noontime came this chap.
Each time he knelt just for a moment, a lunch pail in his lap.
Well, the minister's suspicions grew, with robbery a main fear.
He decided to stop the man and ask him, "Whatcha' doin' here?"

The old man, he worked down the road. Lunch was half an hour.
Lunchtime was his prayer time, for finding strength and power.
"I stay only moments, see, cause the factory is so far away;
As I kneel here talkin' to the Lord, this is kinda' what I say;

"I just came to tell you, Lord, how happy I've been
Since we found each other's friendship and you took away my sin.

TRUE TALES To Live By

I don't know much how to pray, but I think about you everyday
So Jesus, this is Jim checkin' in."

The minister feeling foolish, told Jim that was fine. He told the
man he was welcome to come and pray just anytime.

"Time to go," Jim smiled, said "Thanks."
He hurried to the door.
The minister knelt at the altar, he'd never done that before.
His cold heart melted, warmed with love, met with Jesus there.
As the tears flowed in his heart, he repeated old Jim's prayer.

"I just came again to tell you, Lord, how happy I've been
Since we found each other's friendship and you took away my sin.
I don't know much how to pray,
But I think about you everyday.
So Jesus, this is me checkin' in."

Past noon one day, the minister noticed that old Jim hadn't come.
As more days passed without Jim, he began to worry some.
At the factory, he asked about him, learning that he was ill.
The hospital staff was worried, but he'd given them a thrill.

The week that Jim was with them brought changes in the ward.
His smiles, a joy contagious, changed people, his reward.
The head nurse couldn't understand why Jim was so glad,
When no flowers, calls or cards came, not a visitor he had.

The minister stayed by his bed, he voiced the nurse's concern.
No friends came to show they cared.
He had nowhere to turn.
Looking surprised, old Jim spoke up and with a winsome smile
"The nurse is wrong, she couldn't know, that all the while,
 Everyday at noon, He's here, a dear friend of mine.
He sits right down, takes my hand, leans over and says to me:

'I just came to tell you, Jim, how happy I have been,
Since we found this friendship, and I took away your sin.
I always love to hear you pray, I think about you each day,
And so Jim, this is Jesus checkin' in.'"

A Small Gift of Love

The following story was shared with me by a friend of mine, William Stidger. He had a radio broadcast in New England many years ago. I wrote two stories that he used on his broadcasts. The following incident illustrates how what sometimes seems like a small act of kindness may have unexpected results.

Many people feel that beggars on the street want money only for liquor, but I am sure there are exceptions. This story is about a man by the name of Donley. He had been out of work for several months and had to make his living begging, which he despised.

One cold winter evening, he approached a well-dressed couple and asked for some money with which to buy food. The man ignored him but his wife was more sympathetic.

"Oh, Larry!" she said reproachfully, "We can't eat a meal and not give something to this hungry man out here on the street. I have some change. Let's give him something!" Then turning to Donley, she said, "Here's a dollar. Buy yourself some food. And don't lose courage."

"Thanks, lady," Donley said. "I'll never forget your kindness."

"You'll be eating Christ's bread," the lady said with a smile. "Just pass it on."

Donley found a cheap restaurant and spent fifty cents on the meal, deciding that he would save half of the money for tomorrow. Then he remembered the expression, "Christ's bread." Perhaps he shouldn't keep it all for himself. As he walked out on the street, he saw an old man who looked hungry. He suggested to the man that they go into the restaurant and get something to eat. The old man couldn't believe his good fortune until he found himself seated at a table with a bowl of stew before him.

After he had eaten the stew, Donley noticed that the man was wrapping up a piece of bread in a paper napkin. "Are you saving that for tomorrow?" Donley asked.

TRUE TALES To Live By

"Oh, no," the man replied, "There's a newsboy on the street corner who has had poor luck selling his papers. When I left him, he was crying—I think he's hungry. I want to give him this bread."

The two of them left the restaurant and walked up the street to the hungry boy who thanked the man for the bread and then devoured it hungrily. When he had almost finished eating the bread, he turned to a dog standing nearby, shivering with the cold.

"Here, Jack, you can have some too," he said sympathetically. As Donley was about to leave he noticed that the dog was rubbing against his leg. He bent over to pat it and saw that he had a collar around his neck with a name and address on it. Evidently the little dog was lost. "I must take him to his owner," he thought. After quite a long walk, he arrived at the owner's door and rang the bell.

A man opened the door and eyed Donley sharply. He was about to say, "Did you steal that dog to get a reward?" But he didn't say it. This fellow had an honest look about him. Instead, he said to him, "I advertised in last night's paper. I offered ten dollars reward for the dog. Here is your reward."

Donley looked at the bill with a dazed look, then he said quietly, "I don't want to take the money. I just wanted to do the dog and his master a good turn."

"You take the money," the man insisted. "What you did for me is worth more than ten dollars. Could you be looking for a job? If you are, come to my office tomorrow. I need a man like you."

For two hungry beggars on the street, to a newsboy shivering with the cold, and a lost dog, a kind deed brought amazing results.

The Tiger and the Wise Man

The following is a Korean folk tale but it may well be a true story. Many Korean folk tales were based upon fact.

One day a Korean farmer named Kee called on a blind man who lived in a hut up in the mountains. He was reputed to be very wise. Kee told the wise man that his marriage was once very happy but in recent months his wife nagged him almost constantly. How could he find the happiness he once knew?

"You pull a hair from the tail of a wild tiger and bring it to me," the wise man said, "and I will give you the answer to your problem."

The wise man's answer puzzled Kee. As he followed the mountain path to his home, he shook his head sadly. How could a hair from a tiger's tail possibly make his wife more loving?

After many days of patient search, Kee finally spotted a beautiful tiger. He soon became friendly with the animal by bringing him chicken for food. Eventually Kee became so friendly with the tiger that he succeeded in pulling a hair from the animal's tail. When he presented it to the wise man, Kee was surprised at his advice.

"You be as patient and gentle with your wife as you were with that tiger," he said with a smile, "and you will see a change in her disposition."

It worked! Within a short time, his neighbors noticed that there was no more quarreling at Kee's house. He and his wife again appeared to be a happily married couple. They discovered that a tiger often appeared at Kee's back door, as if begging for a treat. They had no idea that the tiger was in a way responsible for the happy atmosphere in that home.

TRUE TALES To Live By

One day a letter arrived from a minister in Jefferson, Ohio. He had read the story I wrote about the tiger and the wise man. His letter follows:

"The week, after your book arrived with the story about the tiger and the wise man, I was called to a home where a man was very disturbed over his wife's plan to divorce him. He had talked of suicide the night before.

"I listened at some length at the disturbed man's story. Before I left I shared your story of the wise man and the tiger. I have since been counseling with him by phone and in person. Last week he told me about how much progress he has made in building a trust relationship with his wife. With a big smile the man said, 'I'm using the strategy of that story about the tiger. Thank you for your help.'"

I am amazed how the simple story about a tiger was obviously responsible for saving a man's marriage and preventing the husband from committing suicide.

The Lost Bible

A missionary, on leave from China, gave a report in our church on his service in that foreign land. In his message, he told a story I shall never forget.

The parents and children had just completed their breakfast when there was a loud pounding on the door.

"This is the police!" a gruff voice shouted. "Open the door or we'll break it down!" On opening the door, the father found three policemen who pushed him aside and entered the room.

"We want your Bible," one of the policemen demanded. "You are not allowed to have a Bible in your house."

"We won't give you our Bible," the father answered firmly. "You have no right to take it."

"Search the house," the policeman answered with an oath. "We know it's in this house. Find it!" The three men searched all over the house, behind pictures on the wall, under a loose plank in the floor but with no success. Finally, the leader shouted, "Stop it! Beat the man and his wife. Then they will tell." In spite of their cries of pain, they refused to reveal where the Bible was hidden.

Then in desperation, the chief of the police ordered his men to start whipping the children. "Beat them!" he ordered. "They will tell us!" With their hands covering their faces, and shaking under the blows, they refused to tell where the Bible was hidden. Even a little four-year old girl with tears streaming down her cheeks cried out, "I won't tell you. I won't tell you!"

Finally, in disgust, the chief ordered, "It's no use. Leave the house."

All the family knew where the precious Bible was—under a cloth on the kitchen table!

The father gathered his family around him and as they wept tears of joy, he exclaimed, "When our Lord was on earth, He helped the blind people to see. Today, he blinded the eyes of these evil man so they couldn't see!"

What a story! And what a testimony of how even the little children would endure a beating rather than lose the precious book which meant so much to them.

Something for Stevie

This is a story about Stevie, a boy who was mentally handicapped. His employer was a bit concerned after he had hired him. He wasn't sure how his customers would react to Stevie.

He was short, a little heavy, and with the smooth facial features and speech resulting from Down's syndrome.

Stevie's employer wasn't worried about most of his trucker customers because truckers don't generally care

TRUE TALES To Live By

who buses tables as long as the meatloaf platter is good and the pies are homemade.

The four-wheeler drivers were the ones who concerned him; the mouthy college kids traveling to school, the pairs of white-shifted businessmen on expense account who think every truck stop waitress wants to be flirted with. The employer knew those people would be uncomfortable around Stevie, so he closely watched him for the first few weeks. He shouldn't have worried. After the first week, Stevie had the staff wrapped around his stubby little finger, and within a month the truck regulars had adopted him as their official truck stop mascot. After that, the truck stop owner really didn't care what the rest of the customers thought of Stevie. He was a twenty-one year old in blue jeans and Nikes, eager to laugh and eager to please, but fierce in his attention to his duties. Every salt and pepper shaker was exactly in its place; not a bread crumb or coffee spill was visible when Stevie got done with the table.

The only problem was convincing Stevie to wait to clean a table until after the customers were finished. He would hover in the background, shifting his weight from one foot to the other, scanning the dining room until a table was empty. Then he would scurry to the empty table and carefully bus the dishes and glasses onto a cart and meticulously wipe the table up with a practiced flourish of his rag. If he thought a customer was watching, his brow would pucker with added concentration. He took pride in doing his job exactly right, and you had to love how hard he tried to please every person he met.

Over time, it was learned that Stevie lived with his mother, a widow who was disabled after repeated surgeries for cancer. They lived on their Social Security benefits in public housing two miles from the truck stop. Their social worker, who stopped to check on Stevie every so often, admitted they had fallen between the cracks. What Stevie earned at the truck stop was probably the difference between them being able to live together and Stevie being sent to a group home.

That's why the restaurant was a gloomy place that morning last August, the first morning in three years that Stevie missed work. He was at the Mayo Clinic in Rochester getting a new valve put in his heart. His social worker said that people with Down's syndrome often had heart problems at an early age, so this wasn't unexpected, and there was a good chance he would come through the surgery in good shape and be back at work in a few months. A ripple of excitement ran through the staff later that morning when word came that he was out of surgery, in recovery and doing fine. Frannie, the head waitress, let out a war hoop and did a little dance in the aisle when she heard the good news. Belle Ringer, one of the regular trucker customers, stared at the sight of the fifty-year-old grandmother of four doing a victory shimmy beside his table. Frannie blushed, smoothed her apron and shot Belle Ringer a withering look.

"We just got word that Stevie is out of surgery and going to be okay," she explained.

"'I was wondering where he was. What was the surgery about?'" asked Belle Ringer.

Frannie quickly told Belle Ringer and the other two drivers sitting at his booth about Stevie's surgery, then sighed. "Yea, I'm glad he is going to be okay," she said, "but I don't know how he and his mom are going to handle all the bills. From what I hear, they're barely getting by as it is."

Since there had been no time to round up a bus boy to replace Stevie, the girls were busing their own tables that day. After the morning rush, Frannie walked into the boss's office. She had a couple of paper napkins in her hand, and a funny look on her face.

"What's up?" the boss asked.

"I didn't get that table where Belle Ringer and his friends were sitting cleared off after they left, and Pony Pete and Tony Tipper were sitting there when I got back to clean it off," she said. "This was folded and tucked under a coffee cup." She handed over the napkin and three twenty dollar bills fell onto the desk. On the outside, in big, bold letters, was printed, "Something For Stevie."

"Pony Pete asked me what that was all about," she said, "so I told him about Stevie and his mom and everything, and Pete looked at Tony and Tony looked at Pete, and they ended up giving me this." She held out another paper napkin that had "Something For Stevie" scrawled on its outside. Two fifty dollar bills were tucked within its folds.

Three months later, on Thanksgiving, Stevie was scheduled to be back to work. His placement worker said he's been counting the days until the doctor said he could work, and it didn't matter at all that it was a holiday. He called ten times in the previous week, making sure everyone knew he was coming, fearful that he had been forgotten or that his job was in jeopardy. The truck stop owner arranged to have Stevie's mother bring him to work, then met them in the parking lot and invited them both to celebrate his first day back. Stevie was thinner and paler, but couldn't stop grinning as he pushed through the doors and headed for the back room where his apron and busing cart were waiting.

"Hold up there, Stevie, not so fast," his employer said. I took him and his mother by their arms. "Work can wait for a minute. To celebrate your coming back, breakfast for you and your mother is on me."

He led them toward a large corner booth at the rear of the room. Staff members and booth after booth of truck drivers joined the procession to a table covered with coffee cups, saucers, dinner plates, all sitting crooked on dozens of folded paper napkins.

"First thing you have to do, Steve, is clean up this mess," the truck owner said. He tried to sound stern. Stevie looked at him, then at his mother, and then pulled out one of the napkins. It had "Something for Stevie" printed on the outside. As he picked it up, two ten dollar bills fell onto the table. Stevie stared at the money, then at all the napkins peeking from beneath the tableware, each with his name printed or scrawled on it. The truck stop owner turned to his mother. "There's more than ten thousand dollars in cash and checks on that table, all from truckers and trucking companies that heard about your problems. Happy Thanksgiving." But you know what's funny?

While everybody else was busy shaking hands and hugging each other, Stevie, with a big smile on his face, was busy clearing all the cups and dishes from the table.

"Best worker I ever hired," said Stevie's employer.

The Organ Grinder

When I was a small boy—that was many years ago—some tramps would beg for food; others offered to do odd jobs for a meal. I had a friend who told how, when she was a young girl on a farm in rural Minnesota, tramps often stopped at their farm for handouts. When they were not at home, they never locked the door. Her mother would leave a tea kettle on the stove, a tea pot nearby and a plate of cookies on the kitchen table so any tramp passing by could feel free to help himself. They had no fear of anyone stealing something from their home.

At my farm home in Iowa, we occasionally had peddlers stop by. They traveled by foot and carried a bag—like a suitcase—with various items to sell. As children, we looked forward eagerly to the visits of those peddlers. When they opened their bag, in addition to items that were of interest to a housewife, there would always be some toys and candy for the children.

I remember one peddler—he went by the name of Swede John. He owned a store in Fort Dodge, Iowa. Occasionally he went on a trip in the countryside. He did not travel on foot like the other peddlers. He drove a horse and a four-wheeled cart and he had only clothing to sell. My Uncle Will, who lived on a farm near us, always invited Swede John as his guest for the night.

TRUE TALES To Live By

In some communities, there sometimes appeared a *medicine man*. Like Swede John, he had a four-wheeled wagon pulled by a horse, or a mule. He opened up the side of his wagon to fashion a kind of platform, and attracted the folks who passed by with jokes, humorous comments, and puppets. He had medicines to sell, most of which were really of little value but were supposed to cure almost any disease. But he was a great entertainer.

Another different kind of entertainer was a great favorite of mine. He only made appearances at small fairs or carnivals. Known as an organ grinder, he had nothing to sell like the other peddlers. Music was his entertainment, and that was presented through a box mounted on a short pole. He turned a crank attached to the box and it poured forth, especially delightful to the children, the most beautiful music!

That wasn't the only attraction of the hand organ's show. To his delighted audience, sitting or standing in a semicircle around him, there was a little monkey on a leash. He carried a cup into which the folks who were being entertained were encouraged to contribute. The monkey wore a brightly colored shirt, vest and pants and a little cap, and when someone dropped a coin into his cup he would doff his cap as if saying, "Thank you" for the contribution.

ANGELS GAVE THE GIFT OF SONG, AND WHILE ONE SINGS – ONE THINKS NO WRONG.
—*Italian Proverb*

There were adults in the audience too, most of them parents, but it was the children who were especially delighted with the antics of the little monkey who seemed to enjoy his part in the show.

The last organ grinder I had the pleasure of seeing was at the Spencer, Iowa, County Fair. He told me that his father and his grandfather had both been life-long organ grinders.

You would think that being on his legs would be very tiring all day long, but there was something about the happy crowds that followed him that was his reward. The coins that were dropped in the monkey's cup couldn't have been very rewarding, but there was something about the smiles and the laughter of the children that kept him going from one fair to another all of his life.

He said that as far as he knew there were only four organ grinders in the United States who were still following this unusual way of making a living. The music maker and his little monkey have been replaced by the television programs. They are no longer a part of the American scene.

Tolstoy and the Beggar

Leo Tolstoy, the noted Russian author, was strolling along the streets of St. Petersburg one day when a beggar approached him and asked for money with which to buy bread. Tolstoy searched through his pockets but was unable to find even a kopek.

Placing his hand on the beggar's shoulder, he said gently, "Do not be angry with me, Little Brother, but I have no money."

The beggar's eyes lit up, and with a friendly smile he said, "I am not angry with you, kind sir, you have given me more than money."

"But what have I given you?" asked Tolstoy in a puzzled tone of voice.

"You called me, Little Brother," replied the beggar. "That is better than a coin with which to buy bread."

In his latter days, Tolstoy lived among the peasants, and he noticed that, in spite of their poverty, they seemed to

TRUE TALES To Live By

be happy. They had little to eat but black bread. They were devoted to their families, and they loved their homes, although they were very simple with dirt floors and little furniture except a bed, a bench and a table.

One day Tolstoy fell into conversation with a kindly, bewhiskered old gentleman. Said Tolstoy, "My friend, will you tell me the secret of your happiness?"

Replied the peasant in a surprised tone of voice, "You are one of the wisest men in all Russia and you come to me for the secret of happiness?"

"I am not wise," Tolstoy replied. "I am a failure. You teach me."

"You were created by God," the peasant replied. "When you stay in contact with God, joy is continuous. If you get away from God, you get away from joy. Return to God my friend," he said with a gentle smile. "Return to His Son, the Saviour, and you will find good days."

The Old Country Church

By Skip Westphal

There was a little white church in my boyhood days,
Where the country folk gathered to sing their Lord's Praise.
They came with horse and buggy in the warm summer days.
During the deep snows of winter they rode in their sleighs.

In the golden days of autumn, special meetings there would be,
When many found the Lord, it was very plain to see.
It really happened one night to me.

The congregation was singing an old revival song,
The words had been challenging me all the day long.
"I've wandered far away from God, Now I'm coming home.

The paths of sin so long I've trod, Now I'm coming home."

I needed forgiveness for the things I'd done wrong,
That thought gripped my heart like the words of the song.
With a heavy heart I walked down the aisle.
All eyes were upon me, it seemed like a mile.

Searching to find the Heavenly way,
I humbly knelt at the altar to pray.
How long I prayed I do not know
That blessed night so long ago.
But suddenly a joy I had never known
Crept into my heart, I was no longer alone.

I had found a Saviour and a friend
Who would be with me to the end.
I knew if I traveled o'er land and sea
That every day the good shepherd would be near me.

Since that happy eventful day
When the gentle Lord Jesus came by my way,
Many years have passed and gone
But the sweet memory of it lingers on.

There was a time I had the urge to roam,
To Foreign lands far away from home.
At the battlefront across the seas,
To the streets of Paris and New Orleans.
As a circus horseman and a cowhand of the West
My loyalty to my Lord was often put to the test.

Do you wonder why there's a soft spot in my heart
That the memory of that church makes the tear drops start?
What might have been my lot along the way
If the Good Shepherd had not been with me night and day
To guard me and protect me so I would not go astray.

That church no longer stands, its message to tell.
The fields no longer echo to the sound of the bell.
But it lives in my heart and it always will.

TRUE TALES To Live By

How the Great Guest Came

By Edwin Markham

Before the Cathedral in grandeur rose
At Ingelburg where the Danube goes;
Before its forest of silver spires
Went airily up to the clouds and fires;
Before the oak had ready a beam,
While yet the arch was stone and dream
There where the altar was later laid,
Conrad, the cobbler, plied his trade.

It happened one day at the year's white end
Two neighbors called on their old time friend;
And they found the shop, so meager and mean,
Made gay with a hundred boughs of green.
Conrad was stitching with face ashine,
But suddenly stopped as he twitched a twine:
"Old friends, good news! At dawn today,
As the cocks were scaring the night away,
The Lord appeared in a dream to me,
And said, 'I am coming your Guest to be!'
So I've been busy with feet astir,
Strewing the floor with branches of fir,
The wall is washed and the shelf is shined,
And over the rafter the holly twined.
He comes today, and the table is spread
With milk and honey and wheaten bread."

His friends went home; and his face grew still
As he watched for the shadow across the sill.
He lived all the moments o'er and o'er,
When the Lord should enter the lowly door
The knock, the call, the latch pulled up,
The lighted face, the offered cup.
He would wash the feet where the spikes had been,
He would kiss the hands where the nails went in,

SKIP WESTPHAL

And then at the last would sit with Him
And break the bread as the day grew dim.

While the cobbler mused there passed his pane
A beggar drenched by the driving rain.
He called him in from the stony street
And gave him shoes for his bruised feet.
The beggar went and there came a crone,
Her face with wrinkles of sorrow sown.
A bundle of fagots bowed her back,
And she was spent with the wrench and rack.

He gave her his loaf and steadied her load
As she took her way on the weary road.
Then to his door came a little child,
Lost and afraid in the world so wild,
In the big, dark world. Catching it up,
He gave it the milk in the waiting cup,
And led it home to its mother's arms,
Out of the reach of the world's alarms.

The day went down in the crimson west
And with it the hope of the blessed Guest,
And Conrad sighed as the world turned gray:
"Why is it, Lord, that your feet delay?
Did You forget that this was the day?"
Then soft in the silence a Voice he heard:
"Lift up your heart, for I kept my word.
Three times I came to your friendly door;
Three times my shadow was on your floor.
I was the beggar with bruised feet,
I was the woman you gave to eat,
I was the child on the homeless street!"

*Printed with the courtesy of Doubleday and Company, Inc.,
Garden City, New York*

BITS OF HUMOR

SKIP WESTPHAL

Laugh and the World Laughs with You

There are many examples in the writings of great men and women about the importance of a sense of humor. William Makepiece Thackery writes,

> "A good laugh is like sunshine in a house."

Lawrence Sturm expresses his opinion about laughter in these words:

> "I am persuaded that every time a man smiles—
> much more so when he laughs—
> it adds something to the fragment of life."

There is a framed prayer that reads:

> "Bless this house with love and laughter."

● ● ●

The beloved news commentator, Paul Harvey, says, "There are two main reasons for a happy marriage:

1. Both husband and wife be regular attendants at church services.
2. Have a sense of humor."

● ● ●

The following incident is an example of an important truth. How easy it is to worry needlessly about some imagined incident.

An English Archbishop, who was getting quite old, was fearful that one day he would suffer a stroke. One evening he was playing chess with a charming young lady. Suddenly, he slumped back in his chair and uttered a low moan.

"It has come," the Bishop replied in a trembling voice. "My right side is paralyzed."

"How do you know it is paralyzed?"

"I have been pinching my leg," murmured the Bishop, "and there is no feeling in it."

Ah," said the young lady blushing profusely, "Your Grace, I do beg your pardon, but it was my leg you were pinching."

In the jungles of Africa there are many villages where there are no telephones.

On one of my African trips I was accompanied by a missionary, Burleigh Law. We had stopped briefly at an African village but my friend was interested in my meeting the people of another tribe in a village located about ten miles away. He wanted to be sure that the chief would be available so he asked the village drummer to send the following message:

"A man is coming to see you.
He owns a big farm in America and he is a bachelor."

When the drummer was told the words of the message, he looked a bit puzzled. He didn't know the word for farmer or bachelor.

So these are the words he sent out with his drum beats:

"There is a man coming to see you.
He has a big garden in America, and he walks alone."

I have always been amused by the words the drummer used to describe a farmer and a bachelor.

SKIP WESTPHAL

Internationally famous for its ability to eat...
"2,000 MOSQUITOES PER DAY"

In the lobby of the Des Moines, Iowa, Airport, there once appeared a display proclaiming the virtues of the purple martins. On a poster of this unusual bird was a caption beneath it reading,

"Internationally famous for its ability to eat two thousand mosquitoes per day."

The picture is a caricature of a bird sitting at a table. There is a half-filled glass of water on the table and a plateful of mosquitoes. The bird has a knife in his hand and a fork in the other. Impaled on the fork is huge mosquito that the happy bird observes gleefully as he is about to devour it.

It doesn't seem possible that a bird like the purple martin can eat that many mosquitoes a day but that fact is substantiated by J.J. Wade, who heads the Trio Manufacturing Company of Griggsville, Illinois.

Usually we think of the mosquito as a nuisance. But it is more than a nuisance. It is a carrier of fatal diseases. Many dog lovers have grieved over the loss of a pet to an infection caused by a parasite carried by a mosquito. Much more serious than that is the dreaded disease of encephalitis, often referred to as sleeping sickness, which is responsible for many deaths every year. I had a dear friend who died of this dreaded disease. It is well known that the most common carrier of encephalitis is the mosquito.

A realization of this fact leads us to conclude that the friendly purple martins are like flocks of angels that hover over our homes, protecting us from unexpected dangers that may be threatening us.

TRUE TALES To Live By

Three Monkeys

Three Little Monkeys

Three monkeys sat in a cocoanut tree
Discussing things as they are said to be.
Said one to the others, "Now listen, you two,
There is a rumor out that can't be true:
That man descended from our noble race—
The very idea is a disgrace!

No monkey ever deserted his wife,
Starved her babies and ruined her life.
You've never known a mother monk
To leave her babies with others to bunk,
Or pass them on from one to another
'Till they scarcely know which is their mother

Here's another thing a monk won't do—
Go out at night and get on a stew,
Or use a club, a gun or a knife
To take some other poor monkey's life.
Yes, man descended, the ornery cuss,
But brother, he didn't descend from us!"
— Gene Racey

Printed with permission of the author by Westphal Features.

*The author, Gene Racey, has given permission
for the printing of this poem.*

SKIP WESTPHAL

Kiddie Quotes

Any parent will tell you how unpredictable a child can be. The driver of an automobile, stopped by a policeman in London, Ontario, was a young man accompanied by his wife and two children. The policeman was going to write a ticket for speeding, but he put his book away, when a four-year-old, taking the policeman for a waiter, leaned out of the car window and ordered, "Two hamburgers, with mustard and ketchup please."

A Phoenix girl on her fifth birthday opened a card from her aunt and found a one dollar bill inside. Later in the day, a neighbor came over with a card. Inside was another one dollar bill. A disappointed look came over the girl's face. "Aw, gosh," she said, "I've already got one of these!"

A nurse trying to be friendly with a little girl waiting for a tonsillectomy, asked, "Have you ever been in a hospital before?" "Of course," the child is said to have replied, "Where do you think I was born?"

When the telephone rang at a Tucson residence one midnight, the caller said, "There's a package at your door." The homeowner called the sheriff's office first, then looked outside the door. There was a package there, all right, with a note attached. It read, "Please find a home for my babies." It was signed, "Unwed mother." Inside the package were two small, hungry kittens.

• • •

Some days it gets so hot in Phoenix that the only thing a thief will take is an air conditioner. It was on such a day that a man called the newsroom to tell of an incident he insisted had actually happened. He had stopped at a lemonade stand

operated by a nine-year-old boy. There were two lemonade bowls—five cents a glass from one bowl, two cents from another. The man told us he bought two glasses of the two-cent lemonade, then asked the boy how he expected to sell the five-cent lemonade.

"Well," the boy replied, pointing to the two-cent lemonade bowl, "the dog drank out of that one so I thought I had better sell it before somebody found out."

The Ram Had a Sense of Humor

Many of the misfortunes of our daily lives, that are irritating at the moment, later prove to be inconsequential, or even humorous. I was reminded of this truth one day when I listened to a farmer's wife telling of an experience she had had recently with a pugnacious ram. She had gone to the hen house to gather eggs, and was using her apron for a basket. She had collected a couple dozen eggs, and on the way back to the house decided to step into the barn to see if there were any eggs in the cow manger where some of the hens were in the habit of laying.

In the meantime, the old ram had quietly followed her into the barn. His favorite pastime was butting unsuspecting people from the rear. Just as the woman thought, the hens had deposited several eggs under the feed box in the hay. Clutching her bulging apron with one hand, she stooped over to pick up eggs in the manger. As she did so, the eager ram backed up a couple of steps and charged, striking the poor lady hard in the rear. The force of the blow knocked the woman flat on her face on the barn floor. She was not injured, except for her hurt feelings, but all of the eggs in her apron were smashed to a pulp.

For a few moments, the woman sat there ruefully contemplating the mess of broken eggs in her lap. If looks could kill, that ram wouldn't have been long for this world. The animal didn't even show any feelings of remorse about his shameful conduct, but slowly trotted off with his head held high as if he was proud of his accomplishment. Sputtering to herself, the woman finally pulled her self together, gathered up her egg soaked skirt and made her way to the house.

That evening at the supper table, she related her unhappy experience to her family, thinking that they would be very sympathetic about the whole affair. They were so amused at her story, however, that they held their sides with laughter. Then, she, too, began to see the humorous side of the incident and joined with them in their merriment. That incident happened several years ago, and since then my friend has related it scores of times, always in such an amusing manner that her listeners roar with laughter at her escapade.

It's a great gift to be able to look at life's minor irritations in their proper perspective, and to realize that what appears to be a misfortune today, may be an incident to laugh about tomorrow. It was Henry Ward Beecher who said, "A man without mirth is like a wagon without springs in which one is caused to be jolted by every pebble over which it runs."

The Queen Passing By

At a church service in Minneapolis recently, we heard a pastor use a children's story in his sermon from which I thought we all could learn. It was a tale about a peasant farmer in Old Europe who had learned the queen would be passing by his cottage on the following day. He wondered how he should act in the presence of royalty. Should he offer her majesty a gift? Should he salute her, or just what would be the proper thing to do? None of his neighbors had ever seen the queen or her palace so it would be no good to ask them for advice.

TRUE TALES To Live By

Then the thought occurred to him that perhaps some of the birds and animals on his own farm could give him some kind of a clue. He believed that in some respects birds and animals were more intelligent than humans. What human being could travel all the way to the South Pole and find his way back to his home like birds do? What person, after a member of the family has been gone from home for a month, would know—without a letter—that he or she would return home on a particular day like many a dog can do? Anyway, he decided it would be worth a try.

The farmer walked out into his apple orchard to see if he could find a bird he could talk to. He saw an owl perched on the branch of a tree and he said to the owl, "The queen is coming by this way tomorrow and I don't know how I should conduct myself. Do you have any suggestions?"

The owl looked at the man with a stupid expression and replied, "Who?"

"It's the queen," the man replied in an impatient tone of voice. "Haven't you ever heard of the queen?"

The owl stared at him for a moment; then it answered with the same dumb expression, "Who?"

The farmer shook his head in disgust and was about to walk away when he spotted a chickadee sitting on a branch of the tree.

"You look like an intelligent being," the man remarked to the chickadee. "Let me ask you a question. The queen is passing by this way tomorrow. Would it be proper for me to offer her a gift, say a bag of barley?"

The bird didn't stop to think like the owl had done. She immediately replied, "Cheep! Cheep!"

"Now that answer makes sense," the farmer thought. "I'm sure the queen has plenty to eat. She doesn't need a bag of barley. I think I'll walk over to the pasture and ask my horse for advice."

The horse had been munching grass and when he saw his master approaching, he raised his head and whinnied. "Prince," the farmer called out, "the queen will be passing by this way. Would it be proper for me to wave at her?"

The horse shook his head and replied with a snort, "Neigh!"

Now the farmer was getting discouraged. He wasn't getting any help at all. He decided to make one more attempt. Nearby his shepherd dog was guarding a flock of sheep. He called out to her with the same question he had been asking of the owl and the bird and the horse.

"Can you tell me what I should do?" he asked in a desperate tone of voice.

Without hesitation, the dog replied, "Bow!"

The farmer smiled in appreciation, "There!" he exclaimed. "I think that is the answer I have been looking for. "I'll bow to the queen!"

So the next day when the queen appeared in her carriage along the road that led past the farmer's cottage, the farmer stood by the gate with his dog by his side and bowed low to Her Majesty. She waved to him and smiled the sweetest smile. Then she ordered the coachman to stop the horses and for several minutes she visited with the farmer asking him about his apple orchard and his sheep and his cows. Then as she was about to leave she invited him to come and visit her sometime at the palace.

As she drove off, the queen remarked, "That's a beautiful dog you have. She must be a good companion for you."

The dog seemed to understand what the queen had said, for she wagged her tail and barked in appreciation. For a long time the farmer stood by the gate and watched until the carriage had disappeared around a bend in the road. Certainly this had been one of the happiest days of his life!

TRUE TALES To Live By

Humor Lightened Burdens Faced by our Forefathers

Our grandfathers and grandmothers were not sour-faced characters who always looked on the dark side of life. They loved to laugh and share jokes with each other. I can remember my dad, who broke the prairie with three horses and a walking plow, laughed until the tears ran down his cheeks when relating some humorous experience.

Edward Everett Hale was a well-known clergyman of the Revolutionary War days. He was the nephew of Nathan Hale who was executed by the British as a spy and who was famous for his last words, "I only regret that I have but one life to lose for my country." Dr. Hale served as chaplain of the United States Senate. Someone asked him, "Do you pray for the senators, Dr. Hale?"

To which Dr. Hale replied, "No, I look at the senators and pray for the country."

Senator Henry Cabot Lodge of Massachusetts had a great deal of experience serving on investigating committees in the U.S. Senate. He once told the story of a man by the name of Si Hopkins who was hired by the government to shoot the muskrats that were damaging a dam.

"One morning," reported Senator Lodge, "while I was out for a walk, I saw Hopkins sitting on a grassy bank, his gun on his knees. I asked him, 'What are you doing, sir?'"

"I'm paid to shoot muskrats, sir," he said. "They're undermining the dam."

Lodge exclaimed, "There goes one now. Shoot man! Why don't you shoot?" The man puffed for a moment on his pipe, then he drawled, "Do you think I want to lose my job?"

We might ask, "Are there people like Si Hopkins today?"

One of my prized possessions is my mother's scrap book. It contains one hundred pages of poems and stories she often read to us as we sat around the hard coal stove on a cold winter's night. Some of them were inspiring; some very humorous. No doubt our forefathers often told about two Dutchmen, Hans and Jacob. The two men had been up on the roof of a barn all afternoon repairing the shingles. Darkness had fallen before they were aware of it. They suddenly realized, to their consternation, that the ladder on which they depended to descend from the roof had been knocked down—probably by a calf running loose.

"Vot ve should do?" exclaimed Hans in dismay. "If ve chump off der roof, ve break a leg!"

"Dot's no problem," Jacob replied. "Don't you remember dot pile of horse manure at dere end of dere roof. Ve jump into it. It vill be like a pile of straw. I go first."

A moment later, Hans called out, "Yacob, are you OK?"

Jacob replied in a muffled tone of voice, "Don't vorry, Hans. Der manure is only ankle deep."

Summing up his courage, Hans jumped.

A moment later he sputtered, "Vy you say der pile iss only ankle deep. I am up to my neck in manure."

"Der pile iss only ankle deep," Jacob insisted. "I vent in head first!"

Snake in the Clothes Basket

One day in a restaurant in Mesa, Arizona, I had an interesting conversation with a friend who has a story. It was wash day at his home and his wife still likes to dry her washing on a clothesline. She had brought in some clothes and was removing them from the basket when suddenly, to her horror, she uncovered a big bull snake at the bottom of the basket. Her husband who was in the bathroom taking a shower heard her frightened scream for help. He ran from the shower without even taking the time to put on any clothes.

TRUE TALES To Live By

"There was a big snake in that clothes basket," his wife blurted out, pale with fright. "He crawled out of the basket and is now somewhere under that couch."

Getting down on all fours, her husband peered under the couch to see if he could get a glimpse of the snake. At that moment their pet dog appeared on the scene. He was curious to see what all of the excitement was about and was probably puzzled to see his master on his hands and knees in his birthday suit. Suddenly the dog poked his nose against the man's bare bottom. Thinking he was being attacked by the snake, the man let out a loud yell and fell over in a dead faint.

His wife, thinking he had suffered a heart attack from the shock, ran to the phone and called the paramedics. By the time the ambulance arrived, her husband had recovered consciousness. A brief examination showed his heart was normal and the paramedics turned their attention to the job of catching the bull snake. Of all their emergency assignments, I am sure this one was one of the most unusual.

Physical Fitness Not Needed

On the wall of an office that I was recently in, I noticed a sign that reads: "This department requires no physical fitness program. Everyone gets enough exercise:

    Jumping to Conclusions
    Flying Off the Handle
    Carrying Things Too Far
    Dodging Responsibilities, and
    Pushing their Luck

About the Author

Skip at the age of 97, is the author of seven books, twenty magazine articles and over a thousand newspaper stories. He has traveled in sixty countries around the world including five trips to Africa; one of them made possible by the Ford Foundation, a journey to South America, Japan, Korea and Russia.

To get material for his writing, he has worked as a horseman in the Ringling Brothers and Barnum and Bailey Circus, been a sailor on an ocean going freighter and a lumberjack in the Maine woods and ridden on the Pampas of the Argentine. He was a teacher in New Hampshire and in later years farmed the farm upon which he lives.

Among his many adventures, he has been bitten by a poisonous snake, chased by a rhino in the Ngoro, Ngoro Crater of Tanzania.

Skip and his wife Marion are the parents of two adopted Korean daughters.

Skip attributes his success in life to the Lord's guidance in all his undertakings.